Promise and Peril

Promise and Peril

Understanding and Managing Change and Conflict in Congregations

DAVID R. BRUBAKER

THE
ALBAN
INSTITUTE

Herndon, Virginia
www.alban.org

The Alban Institute
2121 Cooperative Way, Suite 100
Herndon, VA 20171

Cover design by Spark Design.

Library of Congress Cataloging-in-Publication Data

Brubaker, David.
  Promise and peril : understanding and managing change and conflict in congregations / David Brubaker.
     p. cm.
  Includes bibliographical references.
  ISBN 978-1-56699-382-1
  1. Church controversies. 2. Change—Religious aspects—Christianity.
  3. Conflict management—Religious aspects—Christianity. I. Title.

BV652.9.B75 2008
250—dc22
                              2008049480

     09   10   11   12   13   VP   5   4   3   2   1

Contents

Foreword

David Brubaker has a significant history working as a consultant to conflicted congregations and other organizations for many years. I first got to know him in a conflict workshop in the 1980s. Over the years I have noted his work and writing. He has made useful contributions to the organizations with which he has consulted and, through his articles, to the literature on conflict in congregations. With this, his first book, he is moving what we understand about conflict, congregational growth and decline, systems theory, leadership, and organizational culture substantially forward. Here he demonstrates a sophisticated understanding of the work of those who have preceded him and, through his research, makes a consequential new contribution to our understanding. He has supported and challenged some of the common wisdom in the field, contributed new insights, and offers wise counsel to those who are involved.

Brubaker says he was motivated to do this research because he felt that the causes of conflict seemed to go beyond what he has seen in other works on similar subjects. He wanted to discover and explore the underlying dynamics of conflict, and he has successfully pushed the envelope of our understanding. He presents a good deal of new material and insights that I believe will reshape some of the common wisdom about churches and synagogues and how they function.

What is particularly appealing to me about this book is that Brubaker has laid out some of the current theories (the common wisdom) of congregational life, developed an instrument to measure what is actually going on in congregations, used that instrument to assess one hundred churches, and then tested current thought against his findings. His reflections are fascinating and useful.

While this approach is not new, we need more books that add research to reflections on the craft of consulting and organization change. Many of the books by consultants on congregational dynamics and conflict are based solely on the reading and experience of the writer. This is not necessarily bad, indeed this approach has produced very useful material; however, we also need writing that is based on a larger perspective. We need assessment based on the experience of randomly selected congregations, in which no consultants have worked, that represent a broad range of sizes, budgets, and settings. Brubaker has provided that for us here.

This book is primarily a description of the author's research and its ramifications on organizational theory. However, to some degree it is also a "how to" book. Brubaker offers useful advice about how to approach change, substantiating his recommendations with his learning from the research. It is out of this mixture of research plus experience plus reflection that Brubaker is able to postulate his "deeper causes," which I find both intriguing and useful.

Within all of this I believe Brubaker has a new slant on trying to figure out what is going on in a conflict. Some of the most popular approaches to conflict start with an assumption as to what the underlying dynamic of conflict is: interpersonal tension, anxiety generated by dysfunctional systems, disagreement about authority, poor communication, competing for scarce resources, attempting to meet unmet needs, etc. Brubaker comes at his subject from a different perspective. He does not presume know the cause of conflict; he only says that there is a correlation between conflict and certain kinds of change, and that it is not just change per se that causes the conflict. He notes that there are changes (even big changes) that happen in congregations that are not associated with conflict. From his research, for example, he observed that in the building of new buildings congregations did not have statistically significant amounts of conflict, contrary to the common wisdom that conflict is indeed associated with building projects both as plans for buildings are discussed and after the buildings are finished. Out of this recognition he surmises that it is the way change is made more than the mere fact that change is occurring that leads to conflict. Plans for constructing or renovating a congregational building, he finds, are among the changes that are more likely to be implemented carefully and cautiously by developing buy-in on the part of the congregation, thus reducing the amount of resistance in the system.

Another very useful observation here is that Brubaker's data did not confirm that conflict inevitably leads to numerical decline within an organization. Another myth bites the dust. Brubaker also found that conflict has different effects on smaller organizations than it does on larger ones.

The reader is not going to find easy answers in this book; indeed, I would say Brubaker complexifies rather than simplifies our understanding of organizational dynamics. I have noted above that some types of change (such as building a new building) are less likely to bring conflict and other types of change (such as a change in governance structure) are more likely to be associated with conflict. Understanding the difference between these two organizational situations helps us learn that change does not necessarily correlate with conflict; whether or not conflict will occur, and to what degree, depends on the change and how that change is handled.

Another similar "complexification" of the common wisdom relates to family systems theory and congregations. Brubaker

recognizes that much of Edwin Friedman's family systems theory is more useful in small (family-sized) congregations than it
is in larger (pastoral-, program-, and corporate-sized) churches
or synagogues. I found this insight to be powerfully helpful in
that I understood Friedman's ideas as a one-fits-all model, which
made my life miserable because I didn't find it useful in many
situations. Friedman's theories gave me a lens to use for the assessment of certain dynamics in congregations, but I found these
insights difficult to apply, especially in large congregations—as
Brubaker confirms.

One of the main insights I have taken from this book is not
one that Brubaker laid out in so many words. He seems to see
conflict not as a problem to be solved in itself, but as a part of
a larger reality in the system. Conflict might be compared to a
fever in the human body. It can be treated per se, but there may
also be something that one does to treat the cause of the fever.
One may work on the conflict (try to improve communication
or get agreement on rules of engagement, for example), but one
may/should also attempt to deal with the problem of which the
conflict is the symptom (by deciding to change the governance
system or the way people worship, for instance).

I do hope David Brubaker will continue to do more of the
kind of research he has done here and will continue to share his
reflections with a wider audience. This book makes a fine and
important contribution to our understanding of religious systems. More books like it would certainly be welcome.

SPEED B. LEAS
Author of *Discover Your Conflict Management Style*

Preface

I had never seen my father in such emotional pain. In 1986 my wife and I returned to Pennsylvania from an overseas service assignment to find my parents immersed in a wrenching congregational conflict. The identified issue was a dispute between my father, who was the senior pastor, and a newly hired associate pastor. The deeper issues seemed to be a history of conflict focused on lead pastors in this congregation and a more recent decision to eliminate the well-established Sunday school classes and replace them with changing elective classes.

The regional judicatory official (a bishop) eventually intervened, along with an outside mediator experienced in congregational conflicts. But sides had already been chosen and conflict escalated, and the intensity of the division soon precipitated the departure of the associate pastor who had maneuvered to eliminate the established classes. Although my father labored on for another year and a half, the conflict ultimately led to his resignation as well. High intensity church conflict had claimed another two victims—and significantly reduced both attendance and giving at this congregation.

Conversations with my father prior to and subsequent to his resignation revealed that he was mostly stunned by the intensity of the conflict and the anger of some of the participants. This was the fifth congregation my father had pastored since becoming a pastor in his twenties, and nothing like this had occurred in the prior parishes. Although he took responsibility for mistakes in hiring and supervising the associate, it was clear that their interpersonal conflict was only one piece of the congregational eruption. I was left with many questions. What else contributed to the mushrooming conflict in this congregation? What were the deeper causes of this conflict? Why was the mediation process ineffective at resolving the conflict?

Several months after returning from our overseas assignment, I began work as the associate director of Mennonite Conciliation Service, based in Akron, Pennsylvania. I had been fascinated by conflict since childhood, mainly because I saw very little overt conflict between my parents but realized it was common in my friends' homes, and eagerly absorbed the tools and skills of mediation and facilitation. I mediated scores of cases referred by local congregations and by the local community mediation center and found great satisfaction in helping individuals reach agreement or at least greater understanding.

In 1987 I intervened along with a local family therapist in my first congregational conflict. The issues focused on leadership, and there was indeed conflict among the leadership team. But again the underlying causes seemed to go deeper, and during the eighteen months that we worked with this case, my colleague and I were able to help the congregation name and begin to change some of the underlying dynamics.

In 1988 I devoured Rabbi Edwin Friedman's classic, *Generation to Generation*, and my congregational consulting practice was transformed. In future congregational cases the emotional patterns and processes became clearer, and I became much more proactive about naming the identified patient phenomenon and the likelihood of pastors and other leaders being cast in this role. I adapted a "history boarding" process to assist congregations in surfacing and naming emotional processes and patterns that had developed over their life spans.

A year later I attended training by former Alban senior consultant Speed Leas titled "Consulting with Severely Conflicted

Churches." In addition to the insights provided by family systems theory, I now had a clear consulting model to use with conflicted congregations, along with a guide to levels of conflict that allowed me to diagnose both issues and conflict intensity before making recommendations for improvement.

The combination of a clear congregational consulting model and a family systems lens improved my success rate in working with conflicted congregations, as did working with a co-consultant (usually female). A colleague and I also developed a "reference team" model, asking congregational leaders to appoint a reference group of six to eight diverse members to accompany the intervention. Between 1987 and 2004 I consulted with nearly thirty congregations and other religious organizations—ranging from Southern Baptist to Episcopal. The interventions ranged from three months to two years in length, but typically averaged nine to twelve months. We would begin with assessment, then develop recommendations, and ultimately assist with implementation and evaluation.

But something was still missing. I wanted to understand the causes of these conflicts, and I was generally offered dozens of explanations during the information-gathering stage of each intervention. The people involved had their own particular hypothesis to explain the conflict, but the most common ones included personality conflicts and communication breakdowns—particularly among the lay or ordained leadership. The simplest explanation—that two or three individuals were most to blame—always seemed to be the most attractive one. I sensed instead that change seemed to correlate with the conflicts, as in case after case a significant change had occurred within the congregation prior to the conflict eruption.

By 2004, when I submitted a dissertation proposal to my committee in the Department of Sociology at the University of Arizona, I wanted to understand more about the relationship between change and conflict in congregations. Although I knew there must be a relationship between these two variables, the literature I reviewed wasn't clear about when change caused conflict or when conflict produced change in organizations—nor what types of change would most highly correlate with conflict.

With my committee's help I developed a seven-page questionnaire designed to elicit from survey participants a list of changes that had occurred in their congregations over the last five years. These included significant numerical growth or decline, changes to worship, a building program, an outreach program, and changes to the decision-making structure. I then included a question about conflict, asking if in the last five years a "conflict serious enough to convene a special meeting or call in outside help" had occurred. If a respondent indicated "yes" to that question, I asked additional questions regarding the nature and outcome of the conflict. In addition, all respondents were asked a series of questions about the demographics (age, size, ethnic composition, and so forth) of their congregation.

The results surprised me, and I think they may you as well. Some changes that have been hypothesized to cause conflict, such as going through a size transition or undertaking a building project, did not significantly correlate in this study. Other changes significantly increased the odds of having a conflict.

I don't doubt that my father and his newly hired associate pastor had a significant personality conflict or that "better communication" might have improved their relationship. I also believe that underlying emotional dynamics in the congregation (that seemed to surface about every seven or eight years and to focus on the pastor) contributed to his departure, as suggested by family systems theory. However, this research suggests that an additional causal factor was the precipitous change to the existing Sunday school classes undertaken by the new associate. Sunday school classes—like worship services—represent a ritualized part of a congregation's culture. And changes to culture, as we will see, need to be undertaken very, very carefully.

Acknowledgments

I would first like to thank my family—Mert, Everett, and Emerson—for their overall support through this project. Studying in a graduate program—and especially completing and revising a dissertation while working—places stress on a family system. Mert and the boys have absorbed that stress with grace and love, for which I will always be grateful.

I also want to thank my dissertation committee—Mark Chaves, Joe Galaskiewicz, and Charles Ragin—for their support and coaching through this process. Mark and Joe, my cochairs, were particularly patient with me, and I appreciate all three for what I learned in their classes as well as during this final stage of the process. Vienna Marum of the Department of Sociology at the University of Arizona was also consistently efficient and helpful as I endeavored to complete a dissertation while 2,500 miles away from Tucson.

In addition, my colleagues in the Center for Justice and Peacebuilding of Eastern Mennonite University (EMU) provided both encouragement and release time so that I could conduct interviews during the 2004–2005 school year and write during the 2005–2006 school year. I am especially grateful to Ruth Zimmerman and Howard Zehr (former codirectors) for their willingness to bring me on faculty while "ABD" and support me through the completion of the dissertation.

I am also grateful to the 101 pastors and priests in Arizona and New Mexico who consented to interviews as I collected data for this project. The great majority of those whom I contacted not only volunteered up to an hour of their time but also consistently shared graciously and openly. In addition, the presbytery executives (Lee Sankey in the Presbytery de Cristo and Ken Moe in the Presbytery of Grand Canyon) and Episcopal diocesan leaders (primarily Bill Greeley, the archdeacon of the Diocese of Arizona) were immediately willing to facilitate my contact with congregations in their judicatories.

There are three more individuals to recognize. Drew Strayer, now an alumnus of the Center for Justice and Peacebuilding, entered the results from all 100 complete surveys into SPSS, a statistical analysis software, while serving as my graduate assistant. Once the Alban Institute had accepted my proposal to turn the dissertation into a book, Alban editor Beth Gaede was extraordinarily encouraging and helpful in coaching me to write for practitioners rather than academics. And Andrea Lee of Legacy Editing provided unusually efficient and professional copyediting services as we finalized the book for publication.

Finally, I would like to thank my parents, Merle and Ila Brubaker, for nurturing my interest in congregations early in life. My father pastored five Brethren in Christ congregations during the first thirty years of my life—two in California, one in Ohio, and two in Pennsylvania. As I discovered by osmosis during those years, congregations are places of both great promise and (at times) great pain. My hope in completing and disseminating this research is that congregational leaders will become more aware of the need for and the potential costs of change in their congregational systems. As this awareness grows, I believe that the promise of congregations will far exceed the pain that is experienced there.

Introduction

More Than a Family System

Congregations matter. More U.S. residents belong to religious congregations than to any other kind of voluntary association. In an era of declining participation in many established associations, 20 to 30 percent of the U.S. population attends weekly gatherings in one of more than three hundred thousand congregations.[1] Significant participation extends well beyond the Bible Belt and beyond Christianity itself. According to Harvard Professor Robert Putnam in *Bowling Alone*, "Faith communities in which people worship together are arguably the single most important repository of social capital in America."[2]

But congregations are important not only for their ability to assemble social groupings but also for the emotional and spiritual impacts on their members and their broader communities. The setting of a local congregation is where the vast majority of U.S. residents ritualize core life events such as birth, marriage, and death. Many individuals report that a small group in their faith community is their greatest source of emotional support, and a congregational conflict can trigger intensely painful personal experiences for those who are emotionally engaged in the conflict. A congregation can be the best of places . . . it can also be the worst.

Congregations are the sites of not only regular praise and worship but also persistent social conflict. Conflict in congregations appears to be nearly as ubiquitous as congregations themselves. Nearly 28 percent of U.S. congregations surveyed through the National Congregations Study (NCS), one of the largest national surveys of congregations, reported experiencing a conflict "for which a special meeting was called" in the previous two years, while almost 27 percent reported that a conflict "led some people to leave the congregation" in the same time period.[3] Although the number of congregations experiencing these serial conflicts is not known, one could safely hypothesize that the majority of U.S. congregations see significant conflict each decade.

Other studies point to even higher conflict rates for congregations. Jack Marcum with the Research Services office of the Presbyterian Church (U.S.A.) compiled data on Presbyterian churches from the Faith Communities in the United States Today study.[4] Marcum found that 79 percent reported "disagreements or conflicts" during the previous five years. Of those congregations, 46 percent described the conflict as either "moderately serious" or "very serious." The most frequently named causes of conflict in these congregations were finances (52 percent), the pastor's leadership (47 percent), worship (45 percent), and "who makes decisions" (42 percent). If finances are viewed as a proxy for a deeper struggle over congregational priorities, then the top four causes of conflict identified for a major subset of congregations in the United States are priorities, leadership, worship, and decision making.[5]

There is evidence that the more serious congregational conflicts can be very costly for affected congregations. I was unable to locate cross-denominational research on conflict outcomes, but 38 percent of the Presbyterian congregations participating in the Faith Communities Today (FACT) study reported that although they resolved the conflict, they had experienced negative consequences such as loss of members. What causes these destructive conflicts?

Former senior consultant with the Alban Institute Roy Pneuman identified nine "predictable sources of conflict" in the congregations with which he consulted: (1) members disagree about values and beliefs; (2) the congregation's structure is unclear; (3) the pastor's role and responsibilities are in conflict; (4) the structure no longer fits the congregation's size; (5) the clergy and lay leadership styles don't match; (6) the new pastor rushes into changes; (7) communication lines are blocked; (8) members manage conflict poorly; and (9) disaffected members hold back participation and pledges.[6]

At least three of Pneuman's sources of conflict relate to organizational *structure* (2, 3, and 4), while another three point to matters of *culture* or practice (5, 7, and 8). The remaining three (1, 6, and 9) involve factors in *leadership and membership,* such as values differences, ineffective change-management efforts, and two issues that are commonly seen as a symptom rather than a cause of congregational conflict—declining participation and pledge rates. Congregational members may indeed be engaged in what they experience as worship wars or power struggles, but these are nested in particular structural, cultural, and environmental contexts.

Change also appears in the organizational literature as a significant variable related to conflict, and change happens in every congregation. As religious congregations change, are they more prone to conflict? For example, when congregations either increase or decrease in size, is conflict more likely to occur? What about other common changes that congregations tend to experience—such as a building program, staff turnover, worship changes, or a change in decision-making processes? This book will explore what kind of changes correlate with conflict and offer tentative theories as to why some changes seem to produce conflict while others do not.

In this book I attempt to bring organizational sociology and congregational conflict together, using the tools of organizational theory and research to understand the deeper dynamics of congregational conflict. My primary purpose is to provide insights and tools for congregational leaders, both lay and clergy, to be more effective change agents and conflict managers. The result, I believe, will be healthier congregations that contribute more effectively to spreading the kingdom of God on this earth.

Congregation as a System

Most of us who work in or with congregations understand that they are organic and interconnected systems. Many of us have gained this insight through a family systems perspective on congregations, thanks to the significant work of writers like Rabbi Edwin Friedman and Rev. Peter Steinke. The family systems lens allows us to view congregations as interconnected emotional systems with particular attention to patterns of anxiety and the critical role of congregational leaders. The introduction of family systems theory (FST) to congregational studies and practice has revolutionized our understanding of congregational systems.

But I believe that an FST lens alone is insufficient to understand complex congregational systems. While FST has great explanatory value for single-cell systems such as family-size congregations, it does not fully explain the complex organizational dynamics of larger congregational systems. Every congregation is indeed an emotional system. But just as individuals are composed of much more than their emotions, so too are congregations. If our theoretical models are limited to a single lens, we should not be surprised when the result is a limited field of view.

In this book I apply general systems theory, as adapted by organizational sociology, to the study of congregations. The general systems approach treats the organization as an organic, interconnected system that includes particular components such as structure, culture, leadership, and environment. Alongside FST, which views the congregation as an emotional system, general systems theory offers language and concepts to also understand the congregation as a social system.[7] Within the interconnected system comprised of a congregation's structure and culture nested in a particular set of environments, leaders and others exercise (and sometimes contest) power and authority. In addition, processes such as change and conflict emerge to challenge the ability of organizational leaders to manage these complex systems. Let's look briefly at the structure, culture, leadership, and environment of a congregation, as well as the change and conflict processes that occur within this system.

Structure

At the simplest level, a congregation's social structure is described in its bylaws and displayed in its organizational chart. The decision-making structure or polity of a congregation may range from congregational (everyone decides) to episcopal (one person decides), but more commonly a board and committee structure make the mundane and the major decisions in congregational life. In addition to its social structure, every congregation also has a physical structure—the physical layout of the buildings, offices, classrooms, and worship spaces that together comprise the congregation's facilities. Much of the interaction patterns of office staff and members can be explained by the physical layout of the congregation's facilities. It is no accident that staff members with adjacent offices tend to connect more than those with offices more distant from each other. Proximity matters.

Two additional variables have a significant impact on congregational behavior and structure—the congregation's age and size. In 1972 the organizational theorist Larry Greiner addressed age by describing five classic phases of the organizational life cycle that loosely correspond to stages of the human life cycle:
1. Entrepreneurial (birth)
2. Collectivity (youth)
3. Delegation (midlife)

4. Formalization (maturity)
5. Collaboration (rebirth or death)[8]

An organization's age, or its point in the life cycle curve, influences its structure, as an organization in the formalization phase will tend to be more bureaucratic than one in the entrepreneurial phase—even when its current size doesn't support the bureaucratic structure. As an example, consider this composite case.

> Historic First Church recently celebrated its 125th anniversary. At its peak in the early 1960s, Historic First welcomed five hundred active members nearly every Sunday. But attendance has declined to barely two hundred souls in the last decade while the decision-making structure has remained unchanged. There are twelve permanent committees in the church, each of which has a chairperson that according to the bylaws must also be a member of the church board. Another six at-large members make the board an eighteen-member body. Finding volunteers to serve on all these committees has become increasingly difficult, and the board has begun to discuss a restructuring process. Put simply, the bureaucratic structure that once served Historic First Church well has become a drain on it today.

This book began as an exploration of the effects of a variety of changes on conflict in congregations, with particular attention to the effect of size transitions. A *size transition* occurs when a congregation moves either above or below its previously established numerical size. In his 1983 book *Sizing Up a Congregation for New Member Ministry,* Arlin J. Rothauge categorized congregations in four groups on the basis of their average Sunday worship attendance. He proposed that a *family-size* congregation numbers up to 50 active attendees, while a *pastoral-size* congregation ranges from 51 to 150. A *program-size* congregation consists of 151 to 350 attendees, and a *corporate-size* congregation has more than 350.

Each of the four categories possesses a unique structure and culture. The *family-size* congregation is a single-cell structure, with one primary group consisting of extended families or "clans" centering on matriarchs and patriarchs. The pastor functions as a chaplain while true decision-making authority is vested in the ruling matriarch or patriarch. In the *pastoral-size* congregation, the pastor is at the center and one or two other (usually part-time) staff assist him or her. The transition from pastoral size to program size (sometimes known as "breaking the 200 barrier") is understood to be the toughest size transition to successfully navigate.

By the time a congregation has reached *program size,* there are generally at least two distinct worshiping congregations (for example, a "contemporary" and a "traditional" service). The pastor functions as a manager and is assisted by several professional staff filling functional roles, such as directing Christian education. The *corporate-size* congregation often has more than two worshiping congregations (multiple cells), and the pastor functions as a chief executive officer, often with "mythic qualities."

My own consulting experience and more recent research indicates a slightly larger set of size boundaries. The following boundaries may currently be more accurate for congregations:
- Family size (up to 75 active attendees)
- Pastoral size (76 to 200 active attendees)
- Program size (201 to 400 active attendees)
- Corporate size (401 to 2000 active attendees)
- Megasize (more than 2,000 active attendees)

A congregation that makes a size transition from pastoral size to program size may need to change the decision-making roles of its pastor, board, and committees—as well as their interaction in the decision-making process. Similarly, a congregation that declines in size from pastoral size to family size can expect conflict over accusations that the "pastor and board make all of our decisions." A size transition could lead to conflict if the decision-making structure failed to adapt to the new reality, and decision making came to be over- or undercentralized.[9] Consider this hypothetical example.

> Green Valley Community Church was founded in the mid-1990s by a very energetic pastor who, as early members remembered, "tended to make all the decisions." As the congregation grew past the "200 barrier," however, centralized decision making became increasingly unwieldy. Although the founding pastor left several years ago and was replaced by a more collaborative senior pastor, the congregation's structure has not yet changed to reflect the change in leadership style. Church staff and committee chairs still bring all major issues to the pastor, despite her protestations that "these are decisions that I don't need to be involved in."

Changes to the decision-making structure of a congregation might also spur conflict. The possible locus of decision making can range from the entire congregation to a single individual. If decision-making responsibility is shifted from its accustomed location to a new one within a given congregation, conflict may result as the previous bearers of authority in the congregational system are replaced by a new set of decision makers. The research summarized in this book explored both possible sources of conflict—the failure to change the decision-making structure as a congregation grew or declined as well as the act of changing the structure.

Culture

Compared to organizational structure, which lends itself to systematic analysis, organizational culture is much harder to assess. This may be partly because members of a congregation have already been influenced by multiple cultural sources before joining a particular congregation. For example, a twenty-something individual will have been shaped by the culture of her family of origin, various academic cultures, and workplace cultures before she makes an adult decision to affiliate with a particular congregation. It can be difficult to disentangle a congregation's culture from the personalities of the many members who comprise the congregation, yet the attempt to do so is usually fruitful.

Even while embracing individuals from multiple cultural contexts, congregations develop their own unique cultures. Organizational culture guru Edgar Schein defines culture as "a pattern of shared basic assumptions that was learned by a group as it solved its problems of external adaptation and internal integration, that has worked well enough to be considered valid and, therefore, to be taught to new members as the correct way to perceive, think, and feel in relation to those problems."[10]

According to Schein, we observe culture in an organization primarily through the visible rituals and artifacts. Rituals are the practices that a congregation undertakes on a regular basis to express its fundamental beliefs. In a Christian congregation, the ritual celebration of communion symbolizes Christ's sacrificial death and his call for us to remember him and to serve each other. Artifacts are the physical symbols that represent a deeper meaning, such as a crucifix on the wall, a pulpit, and an altar. Rituals and artifacts symbolize deeper values and norms that are important to organizational members.

According to Lisa Schirch, professor of conflict studies at Eastern Mennonite University, ritual takes place in a unique social space and communicates through "symbols, senses, and heightened emotions" rather than primarily through words. In short, ritual is "nonverbal symbolic action." When that symbolic action is disrupted through a change in the ritual of worship, conflict may result.[11]

For most religious congregations, the primary experience of ritual—and thus the most visible expression of culture—occurs in the weekly worship service. Within the worship service, music displays both rituals and artifacts. Ritualized ways of singing (from a hymnbook versus words projected onto a screen) are accompanied by artifacts that vary according to the style of music employed (organs and pianos versus drums and guitars). "Worship wars" are thus entirely predictable outcomes from a cultural conflict perspective. When the rituals and artifacts change, congregational members can be forgiven for wondering if deeper level changes to the values and norms are also under way. The research reported in this book also considered conflict that might result from a change to worship—specifically the addition of a praise worship service alongside of an existing service.

Leadership

Many books have touted the importance of leadership to congregational success, and such leaders are presumed to have significant agency—the ability to bring about desired outcomes. Within organizational sociology, however, leaders are understood to have a more nuanced role. One of the primary roles is that of a symbol for the organization. Organizational theorists Jeffrey Pfeffer and Gerald Salancik note that this symbolic role for managers is often constructed with elaborate ritual and ceremony. Some leaders may have very limited influence over outcomes in the organization, but the "very impotence of leadership positions requires that a ritual indicating great power be performed."[12]

For example, universities tend to install their presidents with great pomp and circumstance. From the rituals involved, an observer would surmise that the president is being invested with significant power and authority. Yet conversations with a range of university leaders confirm that university presidents tend to have highly circumscribed power in their systems. Caught between the demands of their boards and outspoken faculty members, university presidents often report that they are negotiators more than deciders. Pastors of program-size and larger congregations often describe a similar phenomenon.

This "manager as symbol" metaphor is not offered to deny the importance of organizational leaders. As Pfeffer and Salancik point out, "important social functions are served by manipulation of symbols."[13] When the coach of the losing football team is fired at the end of the season or the politician who presided over a recession is not reelected, we witness examples of the symbolic power of the leader's role. Organizational leaders are the ones most likely to be praised when things are going well, just as they are to be blamed when things are not.

This perspective on the symbolic role of organizational leaders has its parallel in family systems theory, which emerged from the field of psychology. As developed by Murray Bowen and applied to congregations by Rabbi Edwin Friedman in his classic *Generation to Generation*, family systems theory casts as the "identified patient" the one in whom the stress or pathology of the system has surfaced. Friedman suggests that a pastor, priest, or rabbi is especially vulnerable to being cast as the identified patient because of the tendency of congregational systems to blame all crashes on "pilot error."[14]

But beyond this symbolic role, leaders arguably also have a significant role as change agents within their organizational systems. Management theory, as presented in most business schools in the United States, posits that managers have tremendous agency (if not responsibility) in managing change, culture, and conflict—and virtually every other aspect of modern organizational life. Most management how-to books present qualitative case studies or autobiographies based on one ostensibly very successful leader's start-up or turnaround of a large corporation.

In my consulting experience, organizations tend not to make major changes unless and until their leaders change. Such change may come in the form of replacement of one or more key leaders or in the form of internal changes within the leader or leadership team. A congregation, for example, is unlikely to make significant changes to its worship service as long as the senior pastor is resistant to such changes. Major decisions in congregational life are generally referred to the board (or the vestry or session) on which the pastor or priest sits and over which this leader often presides. If the leader is opposed to or uncomfortable with the proposed change, it is normally denied or at least deferred.

Imagine a program-size or larger congregation with a typical board structure where a staff member is proposing a change to the worship service. Before the proposed change comes to the board, it will likely have been processed by the worship committee and approved by the senior pastor. If the senior pastor does not personally sponsor the proposed change, board members will likely inquire as to his or her support for the recommendation. Regardless, the senior pastor and the staff person will generally be seen as responsible for the change.

If the change is seen as successful and is broadly supported by the congregation, those leaders will likely receive much of the credit for that change. If the change is viewed as unsuccessful and is opposed by at least a significant segment of the congregation, the leaders will likely receive much of the blame for the change.

Leaders, then, are both actual agents for change and the symbolic representatives of that change within their congregational systems. When the team has a winning season and the stands are full, the leader is likely to be praised for foresight in implementing the "needed changes." But if the season is unsuccessful and the stands are half empty, one might expect calls for the coach to be fired and replaced with someone who has a better track record. Leaders are agents, but they are also symbols. Leaders initiate change within their organizations, and then they quickly become the primary symbols of that change. In the research, I explored the relationship among change, conflict, and the departure of pastoral staff.

Environment

In addition to structure, culture, and leadership, a fourth variable of interest to organizational sociologists is the environment.

Organizational sociologists view an organization as nested in a complex set of overlapping environments. At the simplest level is the geographic location of the organization. Congregation members normally describe this environment as the community that surrounds the congregation. As sociologist Nancy Ammerman has found, when a community grows, declines, or changes in composition, the congregation is likely to be significantly affected.[15]

Beyond the immediate geographic community lies the institutional environment described by sociologists Walter Powell and Paul DiMaggio.[16] For a local congregation, this environment will generally include the denominational structure in which it is nested (Presbyterian, Episcopal, Mennonite, and so forth), as well as local and national congregations and religious movements that affect congregation members. In the current U.S. religious landscape, the impact of megachurches (churches with two thousand or more people in regular attendance) and their highly visible lead pastors are a significant feature of the institutional environment.

Finally, all organizations are immersed in social, cultural, legal, political, economic, technological, and physical environments. For U.S. congregations, social and cultural changes including the decline of the "traditional family" and rising consumerism are particularly relevant environmental changes. The political environment in this country has been generally favorable to formal religious organizations, but the economic environment exerts pressure to increase the salaries and benefits of the professional staff that serve congregations and to upgrade the facilities. Finally, revolutionary technological changes in the environment are dramatically affecting congregations, prompting both requests to turn off cell phones and the increased use of visual and auditory media during worship.

As congregations adapt to changing environments, they experience internal changes as well. One branch of environmental theory, known as population ecology, applies Charles Darwin's survival of the fittest argument to organizations, noting that organizations that fail to adapt to a changing environment will be selected out. In reality, most congregations are continually making adaptive changes to their facilities, programs, and staff in order to remain relevant to a changing environment. Thus, the subject of congregational change also needs to be considered. This research examined changes in congregational environments to see if those changes might predict congregational change and conflict.

Change

For the past twenty years, a common theme in the literature of the sociology of religion has been that North American religion is undergoing a significant restructuring or transformation. Robert Wuthnow suggests that denominationalism is fading in significance, Mark Chaves contends that religious authority is declining, and Amanda Porterfield concludes that a "post-Protestant culture" is emerging.[17] Theorists attribute such transformations to broader shifts in U.S. society, including the fading influence of the World War II generation and the increasing ethnic and religious diversity of the country.

Although organizational sociologists agree that organizations tend to adapt to their environments, they have used a variety of terms to describe this change—including *transformation*, *restructuring*, and *evolution*. They have also attempted to measure such changes at a broad range of levels—from the society to a denomination to a particular congregation. DiMaggio and Powell offer the clearest definition of organizational change: a "change in formal structure, organizational culture, and goals, programs or mission."[18] In short, when an organization changes its structure, culture, or strategies, we can declare that organizational change has occurred.

Consistent with the scholarly work on organizational change in a changing environment, numerous books designed to appeal to congregational leaders have appeared in the past fifteen years. Titles include *Navigating the Winds of Change, Leading Change in the Congregation*, and *Redeveloping the Congregation*.[19] Most striking about these titles is the extent to which they incorporate and popularize themes developed in the social science and management literature, such as John Kotter's "eight-stage program for lasting change."[20]

One of the most consistent themes of these popular books is that changing an existing congregation is very difficult. One author cites the conventional wisdom that it is "ten times easier" to plant a new church than to change an existing one. Established congregations, especially mainline Protestant ones, are generally viewed as obdurate institutions that become amenable to change only with great exertion from internal leadership or at a time of leadership transition. Congregations, at least from the perspective of those who write for practitioners, are places of remarkable stability rather than rapid change. Disrupting the homeostasis of these organic systems is seen as a highly risky—if sometimes necessary—activity of congregational leaders. In addition to the structural and cultural changes described above, this research explored a variety of other changes in a congregation and their relationship with conflict, including building projects.

Conflict

The study of conflict in religious organizations also claims a long heritage. From Georg Simmel's striking century-old observation about church conflict ("because of dogmatic fixation, the minutest divergence here at once comes to have logical irreconcilability"), to Dean Hoge's 1976 study of *Division in the Protestant House* and Hugh Halverstadt's more recent *Managing Church Conflict*, the phenomenon of conflict in supposedly bucolic church settings has attracted sociological and theological interest.[21]

Mennonite sociologist Fred Kniss applied social movements literature to religious conflict. Kniss found that the key variables in determining the outcomes of intra-Mennonite conflicts were factors inside the movement and the denomination instead of the content of the conflicts themselves. One of the factors that seemed to play the most significant role in conflict outcomes was the contending parties' degree of organization (measured, for example, by the presence of identified leadership).

In assessing five possible outcomes for groups challenging the leadership or initiating a conflict—withering, defeat, schism, compromise, and victory—Kniss found that when an "organized challenger" confronted an "organized defender," schism was most likely. Kniss's findings would suggest that the more organized are the movement and countermovement within a given denomination or congregation the more likely will be high-intensity conflict or even division.[22]

Episcopal author Mary Lou Steed also studied church schism through an analysis of the formation of secessionist congregations within the Episcopal Church over the issue of ordination of women and a revision to the Book of Common Prayer. Qualitatively comparing four cases, Steed concludes that a leader who functions as a pastoral bishop, as opposed to a prophetic or an administrative one, reduces the likelihood of secession. Although the small number of cases in Steed's study makes generalizations quite tentative, the important factor of organizational leadership in conflict merits more scholarly attention.[23]

From this brief review of the literature, organizational conflict has often been portrayed as a dependent variable upon which various other factors—including power, structure, culture, and leadership—have an effect. Of course, conflict itself can have a reciprocal effect on these variables—leading to changes in power relations, organizational structure or culture, and which persons hold leadership roles. This difficulty in determining the causal direction of conflict—when it is an effect of other organizational changes and when it is a cause of such changes—means that it is essential to know when the changes and the conflict occurred. Without knowledge of the time sequence within which change and conflict occurred, establishing causal direction would be impossible.

Chapter Outline

This book summarizes the findings of a quantitative study of 100 congregations in a rapidly changing environment and their experiences of change and conflict. I first identified a population of approximately 140 Presbyterian and Episcopal congregations located in the dynamic environment of the southwestern United States. Clergy and lay leaders from about 70 percent of the congregations (100) were available and willing to participate in the study. In the following chapter, I discuss both the original research questions regarding size transitions and conflict and the strong correlation between conflict and both changes to worship and changes to decision-making structure.

The following three chapters discuss key aspects of the findings in greater detail. Chapter 2 offers a possible mechanism by which changes to a congregation's decision-making structure might translate into increased risk of congregational conflict, particularly exploring the importance of power dynamics. Chapter 3 does the same regarding changes to worship, suggesting that disruption of ritual may explain the correlation with conflict. Chapter 4 examines the key roles of ordained leaders in religious congregations, noting their role as both agents and symbols of change.

In chapter 5, I develop a theology of change and conflict that goes beyond the social science literature and research to offer guidance from Scripture and the early church for proactive change efforts that diminish rather than escalate destructive conflict. Knowing that changes to worship and decision making correlate with conflict should not deter congregational leaders from undertaking such changes. Rather, they need to be initiated in ways consistent with the congregation's deepest values and norms and in the light of guidance from its beliefs and traditions. In the concluding chapter (chapter 6), I summarize the findings from this study and offer suggestions for congregational leaders who desire to be effective managers of both change and conflict.

Congregations matter. Despite declining participation rates since the 1950s, they continue to gather more U.S. residents on a weekly basis than any other voluntary association. And the persistence of conflict within many religious congregations has spawned a conflict-management industry focused entirely on congregations. Lacking, however, has been significant empirical investigation of the causes of such conflict as well as effort to apply these learnings to real-life congregations. This book represents one attempt to address this significant gap.

CHAPTER 1

Overview of the Study

What causes conflict in congregations? When a congregation undertakes a major building project, does conflict follow? What about worship wars—does the introduction of a more contemporary service spark conflict? Given the polarized political environment in the United States, are political differences within congregations a major cause of conflict? Or is conflict caused more by theological variations, particularly differing views of Scripture on issues such as homosexuality and abortion? Perhaps it is caused by power struggles or by changes to a congregation's decision-making structure. Or is conflict more a product of anxious and nondifferentiated congregational leaders?

Aside from anecdotal evidence collected by congregational consultants with significant experience in conflicted congregations, little empirical research exists regarding what causes conflict in congregations.[1] The study reported in this book used the tools of quantitative survey research and statistical analysis to understand the phenomenon of congregational conflict.

To study any social phenomenon, researchers first have to identify a population of individuals or groups where the phenomenon might be occurring. Because of my interest in the relationship between change and conflict, I chose to focus on congregations located in the southwestern United States—a region that has grown rapidly in the past fifty years—and particularly in the state of Arizona.

Between 1950 and 2000, Arizona's population mushroomed from under one million to more than five million—a 500 percent growth rate. With the exception of Nevada, no other U.S. state offers a more rapidly changing environment in which to study congregations. And because I had resided in Arizona for twelve years at the time the study commenced and had developed relationships with judicatory officials, I knew that I would have access to congregations in that state through these gatekeepers.[2]

My goal was to secure participation in the research project from at least one hundred congregations holding membership in either the Presbyterian Church (U.S.A.) or the Episcopal Church.[3] I chose to study Presbyterian and Episcopal churches because their congregational governance structures (polity) are functionally similar, and polity differences were not the focus of this research. A lay board that includes the pastor or priest (called a "session" in Presbyterian congregations and a "vestry" in Episcopal ones) governs each congregation. Although under canon law the Episcopal diocesan bishop possesses more authority than the Presbyterian executive presbyter, in practice the bishop often relates to local congregations in an advisory capacity similar to that of the bishop's Presbyterian counterpart.

The congregations in the study were affiliated with one of three local judicatories (regional governance structures)—the Presbytery of Grand Canyon, the Presbytery de Cristo, and the Episcopal Diocese of Arizona. I used a three-step approach to congregations within the target population:

1. Initial letter of introduction regarding the research project, including a sample copy of the phone survey with a cover letter from the judicatory official
2. Follow-up phone call for the purpose of scheduling a time to conduct a phone interview with a key informant from the congregation

3. Estimated forty-five-minute scheduled phone call to
   conduct the phone interview

My strategy was to always ask first to speak with the lead pastor, but if the pastor were not available I attempted to complete
the survey with a leading ordained or lay member of the congregation—preferably the associate pastor or chair of the governing
board. In most cases I was able to secure an interview appoint-
ment after one or two attempts to contact the lead pastor. If I was
unable to have direct contact with him or her, my protocol was
to leave a maximum of three messages. If the lead pastor did not
return my call after three attempts, I discontinued my effort to
make contact.[4]

The phone interviews were conducted between October
2004 and April 2005. (See appendix A for the interview questions.) After completing the survey, I analyzed the data using
statistical analysis software called SPSS (Statistical Package for
the Social Sciences). The results that follow are a summary of
the findings from the survey. This chapter contains the general
findings; the three most significant implications are explored
in the following chapters.

Demographics

The mean founding date of the surveyed congregations is 1950,
meaning that the average congregation was about fifty-five years
old at the time of the study. The mean attendance (as of 2004)
was 209 and the median was 130,[5] with the smallest congregation reporting 15 active year-round attendees and the largest
1,300. Of the 100 congregations surveyed, 25 were family size
(up to 75 attendees), 40 were pastoral size (76–200), 23 were
program size (201–400), and just 12 were corporate size (401
and larger).[6] Nearly two-thirds of the congregations averaged

Figure 1.1. Distribution of congregations in the research sample across congregational size categories.

Family size (up to 75)	25%
Pastoral size (76–200)	40%
Program size (201–400)	23%
Corporate size (401–2,000)	12%
Megasize (2,001+)	0%

200 or fewer people in weekly attendance. Respondents estimated that their congregations were, on average, 60 percent female and 40 percent male.[7]

Perhaps the most striking implication of these demographic descriptors is how ordinary this population of congregations appears to be—at least for mainline Protestant congregations at this point in U.S. history. The average congregation was midsize (about 200 active members), middle-aged (organizationally), and predominantly female (60 percent) and white (nearly 87 percent). Lay leaders were also middle-aged (56 years old on average), and the ordained pastor was highly likely to be male (87 percent of pastors in this sample). This ordinariness may also mean that

Figure 1.2. Mean and median congregational age, size (attendance), and budget for 100 congregations surveyed.

Congregational Age
    Mean: 55 years
Year Founded
    Mean: 1950   Median: 1957
Congregational Worship Attendance
    Mean: 209 people   Median: 130 people
Congregational Budget
    Mean: $359,000 ($1,717/member)
    Median: $200,000 ($1,538/member)

the results can be generalized—at least to other predominantly European American mainline Protestant congregations.

Consider this composite of the average congregation in the study:

> The Placid Meadows congregation was established in the
> 1950s in what was then a newly developing subdivision on
> the far outskirts of Phoenix. It grew rapidly the first twenty
> years, hitting an average attendance of 200 in the mid-1970s.
> Attendance peaked at 300 in the 1980s and has declined
> somewhat the last twenty years but remains around 200 today.
> The congregation's budget is supported in part by endowments
> left by several of the congregation's founding members.

Structure

About three-quarters of these congregations reported some sort of shared-leadership model, meaning that the board and the pastor or priest shared leadership, and a majority also had written job descriptions for staff and personnel policies. Again, the ordinariness of these congregations is apparent—at least for established mainline congregations that are expected to have a decision-making structure involving some sort of power sharing between the clergy and the laity.

> Placid Meadows developed job descriptions for its four staff
> positions about ten years ago. The session also has been
> recently discussing the need for a job description for session
> members and a written organizational chart that would show
> lines of accountability. The pastor reports that the "session
> leads the church" but acknowledges that he is part of the
> session and exercises a lot of influence in session discussions.

Figure 1.3. Percentage of congregations with written policies and
  formalized governance structure.

Job descriptions	86% of congregations
Personnel policies	58% of congregations
Organizational chart	38% of congregations

Culture

By far the most significant opportunity for affiliation within the
congregations is the weekly worship service. The worship service
is at the center of this group of congregations' corporate experience, which is the case for nearly all Christian congregations.
Worship attendance is also the standard by which congregational
participation is measured, and all other affiliation opportunities
represent some fraction of that total. Finally, more congregations
identified with their denomination as a primary source of identity than with their community.

> Placid Meadows sees itself as a rather typical Presbyterian
> congregation that is somewhat involved with its presbytery
> (judicatory). Although the congregation's facility is located in a
> growing suburban community outside of Phoenix, the pastor
> reports that people attend the congregation either because
> they like the worship service or because they are seeking a
> Presbyterian church and this was the closest one available.

Figure 1.4. Affiliation in activities other than worship as a
  percentage of average worship attendance.

Adult education	31.4% of adult attendees
Board or committees	26.7% of adult attendees
Small group meetings	22.4% of adult attendees

Leadership and Environment

The mean number of full-time staff in these congregations was 2.5, and the mean tenure of senior pastors was 7.5 years.[8] Thirteen percent of the senior pastors were women, slightly higher than the national figure of 10 percent.[9] The mean age of board members was 55.8 years, although it ranged from a low of 42 in one congregation to a high of 70 in another—the latter for a congregation located in a retirement community.

The great majority of the congregations are located in dynamic environments characterized by population growth (61 percent) and changes in ethnic composition and in employment opportunities in their communities. A majority of respondents (59 percent) also reported either some expansion or significant expansion by other Christian churches in their immediate area. The areas least likely to be described as "growing" by respondents were larger urban areas; rural communities, smaller urban areas, and suburban communities were consistently described as growing.

Pastor Smith has been the lead pastor at Placid Meadows for just a bit over seven years and supervises one other full-time staff person—an associate pastor. In addition, a secretary and a youth minister both serve on a half-time basis. The suburban

---

Figure 1.5. Staff numbers, pastoral tenure and gender, board-member age.

Number of Full-Time Staff
    Mean: 2.5 staff   Median: 1.0 staff
Tenure of Lead Pastor
    Mean: 7.5 years   Median: 6.0 years
Female Lead Pastor: 13% of congregations sampled
Mean Age of Board
    Members: 55.8 years

community where Placid Meadows is located experienced significant growth in the last 20 years, and Pastor Smith has noticed a growing number of independent congregations expanding in the community.

Change

Despite rapid population growth in Arizona, less than half of the congregations (42 percent) experienced numerical growth in the five-year period covered by the survey, while the majority (54 percent) remained stable, experienced decline, or did not have sufficient data to determine growth or decline (four congregations). Mean attendance among the participating congregations declined slightly from 214 in 2000 to 209 in 2004, an average loss of one attendee per congregation per year. Presbyterian congregations were slightly more likely to report growth (45.8 percent) than were Episcopal congregations (40.5 percent) during the five-year period studied.[10]

Exactly three-fourths of the congregations experienced turnover of paid staff positions during the five-year period. Only 18 percent of the congregations experienced a "size transition," meaning that they either grew above or declined below a previ-

---

Figure 1.6. Congregations making size transitions

Transitioned between family and pastoral size	4 up, 4 down
Transitioned between pastoral and program size	4 up, 4 down
Transitioned between program and corporate size	1 up, 1 down
Did not transition	78
Insufficient data	4

Figure 1.7. Growing and changing congregations.

Initiated community outreach	65%
Initiated building projects	46%
Growing congregations	42%
Added or deleted a worship service	42%
Experienced a size transition	18%

ous size category.[11] Given that less than one-fifth of the sample experienced a size transition, the overall trend seemed to be one of relative stability in attendance patterns.

About two-thirds (65 percent) of the congregations initiated new community outreach programs between 2000 and 2004, while more than half (57 percent) of the congregations also began new programs within the congregation, ranging from children's programs to adult cell groups. Nearly half (46 percent) initiated a building project in the five years of the study, 42 percent added or deleted a worship service in the same time period, and only 13 percent of the congregations reported that they had made other "significant changes."

By and large the survey results paint a picture of a population of congregations that are changing—although not necessarily growing. Although the result may seem counterintuitive, there was no correlation between building projects and attendance growth in this sample of congregations during the five-year period studied. Of the 46 congregations that undertook a building project, 22 reported growth and 24 reported either no growth or decline. Congregations might have built or remodeled in the expectation that this would draw new people, but those expectations were not consistently supported—at least in the short run.

As the popular literature on congregational transformation suggests, it appears that when it comes to attendance most congregations are remarkably stable institutions. Congregations may change their pastors, their programs, and even their buildings with some regularity. They are less likely, however, to abruptly change their attendance patterns.

> Although Pastor Smith devoted much of his first two years
> to getting to know the congregation, the last five years he
> has encouraged the session to develop a variety of new
> ministries and outreach programs. With the leadership of a
> small group of committed lay members, the congregation
> began a ministry to mothers of preschoolers five years
> ago, and experimented with the Alpha program (to reach
> unchurched members of the community) last year. This year
> the session's priority is exploring the feasibility of building a
> new sanctuary and transforming the current sanctuary into
> a fellowship hall and recreation center.

Conflict

Of the 100 congregations surveyed, 45 percent reported they had experienced at least one conflict "significant enough to convene a special meeting or call in outside help" during the five years of the study.[12] Interestingly, the Presbyterian and Episcopal subgroups experienced conflict at virtually the same rate during that time period. In any given year, approximately 10 percent of the congregations were embroiled in a significant conflict. Eleven congregations—nearly a quarter of the conflicted congregations—reported that they had experienced two or more conflicts over the previous five years. The conflict intensity averaged 3.35 for those reporting only one conflict and 3.5 for those reporting a second.[13]

When asked to identify the principal parties to the conflict, 67 percent of respondents reporting a single or first conflict said "the pastor," 47 percent identified "key families," and 44 percent pointed to board members. Regarding the primary issues that

Figure 1.8. Conflict patterns in 100 congregations studied.

Experienced conflict	45% of congregations
Average intensity	3.35 (Leas scale)
Principal party	Pastor (67% of cases)
Principal issue	Leadership (48% of cases)
Common outcome	People left

were in dispute, 22 of the 45 respondents reporting a single or first conflict said "leadership," 10 identified "homosexuality," and 8 said either "personalities" or "finances." The outcome of a single or first conflict generally involved people leaving—usually certain lay members (in 73 percent of the conflicts) and/or the pastor or other staff (in 32 percent of the conflicts).[14] In 21 percent of the single or first conflict cases, however, losses were relatively minor or the situation actually resulted in improved procedures or processes. By and large, congregations that experienced conflict relied on congregational or denominational resources for assistance.[15] When congregations in this sample fought, they preferred to keep it within the extended family.

Pastor Smith's greatest challenge came about two years ago, when he had been at the congregation for five years and had made a commitment to serve for at least another five. Several disgruntled lay members, including two session members, began to grumble about Pastor Smith's "lack of leadership." The main allegation seemed to be that if Pastor Smith were providing genuine leadership, the congregation would be growing. Pastor Smith met privately with the concerned members, and a special meeting of the session was called to deal with the conflict. Most session members supported Pastor Smith's leadership, but two families (including one of the upset session members) left the church as a result of the conflict.

General Observations

Larger congregations were more likely to report growth during the previous five years than were smaller congregations. While 50 percent of the program- and corporate-size congregations reported attendance increases in the previous five years, only 35 percent of family-size congregations and 44 percent of pastoral-size congregations experienced growth. The size of a congregation does matter—at least when it comes to growth.[16]

Despite the current emphasis on mission-driven churches, as indicated by the plethora of consultants, seminars, and books on the topic, the mere existence of a mission statement did not significantly correlate with growth. Overall, 53 percent of congregations with a posted mission statement reported no growth over the five-year period surveyed, about the same as the overall proportion.[17] Congregations that identified more with the surrounding community than with their denomination were slightly more likely to report growth than those congregations whose respondents indicated a more denominational identity. However, no statistically significant correlations existed between any indicator and a dummy variable established to measure church growth.

Of the 30 conflicts reported to be about the pastor, 47 percent took place in pastoral-size congregations (compared to 13 percent in family-size and 20 percent each in program- and corporate-size congregations).[18] In other words, pastor-centered congregations were significantly more likely to experience a conflict focused on the pastor.

The most striking observation is that the congregations least likely to be growing—family-size congregations—were also the ones *least* likely to experience a conflict, whereas the congregations most likely to be growing—corporate size—were the ones *most* likely to report a conflict. Congregations in suburban and small urban settings also experienced conflict at a higher rate than did congregations in rural and large urban settings, perhaps due to the fact that in Arizona these environments tend to be growing more rapidly. Congregations that reported conflict were only slightly less likely to report growth in attendance than those that did not experience conflict (41 percent versus 45 percent). Thus, a conflict experience per se did not seem to be a significant deterrent to congregational growth.

General Impressions

- Smaller congregations report older session members.
- Smaller congregations are overrepresented in rural and small urban communities.
- Smaller congregations are less likely to grow.
- The existence of a mission statement does not correlate with growth.

In part because of the pressure from the disgruntled lay members for "more growth," Pastor Smith has encouraged the session to try several new mechanisms that might lead to church growth. The associate pastor was familiar with the Alpha program from a previous congregation she had served, and she led initial meetings last year that were moderately successful at attracting participants but did not result in any new members. The session went through a strategic planning retreat two years ago that produced a revised mission statement and a new vision and goals, the first of which was "to grow to at least 300 active members to better serve Christ and our community." However, the congregation continues to average just below 200 persons in attendance at Sunday worship year-round.

Change and Conflict

Within this sample of 100 congregations, four specific changes correlated significantly with conflict. This does not necessarily mean that these changes *caused* the conflict. Rather, they suggest that conflict tends to be associated with these changes in a statistically significant way.[19] These four changes were as follows:

1. Changes to decision-making structure. The correlation of changes to decision-making structure with conflict was .377, meaning that when congregations changed their decision-making structures they were also moderately likely to have experienced a conflict (during the previous five years).
2. Turnover among pastoral staff. There was a correlation between staff turnover and conflict, at a moderate rate of .312. This suggests, not surprisingly, that congregations that experienced conflict were also more likely to experience staff turnover during the previous five years.
3. Adding or dropping a worship service. Congregations were far more likely to add a worship service than to discontinue one, but taken collectively the correlation with conflict was .292, meaning that, again, congregations that added or dropped a worship service were moderately likely to also have experienced a conflict in the previous five years.

Figure 1.9. Correlation of selected changes with conflict.

Changes to decision-making structure	.377 Correl. (sig. at .01)
Turnover among pastoral staff	.312 Correl. (sig. at .01)
Adding or dropping a worship service	.292 Correl. (sig. at .01)
Changes in fellowship patterns	.221 Correl. (sig. at .05)

4. Changes in fellowship patterns. Congregations that changed their fellowship patterns (such as adult education classes or small groups) also demonstrated a correlation with conflict, albeit at a relatively low rate of .221. (For more detail, see the table in appendix B, "Correlations between Conflict and Key Independent Variables.")

After discovering these correlations, I then conducted a statistical analysis to see what correlations would be significant when other relevant variables were included in what statisticians call a multivariate regression analysis. When researchers conduct a multivariate regression analysis, they are simply including a number of possible variables to see which remain significantly correlated with the variable of interest (conflict, in my case). My regression model included six change variables and four control variables. Six of the change variables that were requested in the survey were included to test the effect of various changes on conflict:

- Turnover in a full-time staff position
- Addition or deletion of a worship service
- A new building project, including a major renovation
- A dummy variable for occurrence of a size transition[20]
- Reported changes to the congregation's decision-making structure
- Actual change in attendance between 2000 and 2004

The four control variables I used in the model were congregational size (measured by attendance in 2000), congregational age (years since founding), the tenure of the senior pastor, and denominational affiliation (Presbyterian or Episcopal). Size and age are two classic organizational variables, and the tenure of the senior pastor and denominational affiliation seemed to be logical additional choices for control variables.

The control variables are included to account for the possibility that the variations among the congregations are due to basic differences among them and not to the changes they experienced. By controlling for these four variables, I was attempting to ensure that the differing outcomes found in the sample were actually due to the changes experienced, not to the differing nature of the congregations themselves.

For those who understand and enjoy regression analysis, the full results can be found in appendix C, "Logistic Regression—Full Model." For the majority of us who are instead "statistically challenged," only two changes remained significantly correlated with conflict when the full regression model was tested. These changes are as follows:

- Changes to decision-making structure (significant at the .05 level)
- Adding or deleting a worship service (significant at the .05 level)

If a congregation made either change in the five-year period of the study, they were 3.3 times more likely to also experience a conflict (compared to congregations that did not make such a change). If they made both changes in that period, they were 7 times more likely to experience a conflict.

To further analyze the effect of growth or decline on conflict, I organized the cases into four categories based on the size of the growth or decline that was reported during the five years requested by the study. Congregations that added from 1 to 50 attend-

Figure 1.10. Correlation of growth and decline with conflict.

Significant decline (n=14)	78.6% experienced conflict
Significant growth (n=9)	55.6% experienced conflict
Modest decline (n=33)	42.4% experienced conflict
Modest growth (n=31)	41.9% experienced conflict

ees between 2000 and 2004 I classified as "modest growth," and those that declined by 1 to 50 attendees during the same period were classified as "modest decline." Congregations whose growth exceeded 50 attendees I categorized as "significant growth," and those whose decline exceeded 50 attendees were categorized as "significant decline." The results indicate that conflict was somewhat more likely among the congregations that experienced "significant growth" but much more likely among those that experienced "significant decline."

> In his efforts to encourage growth at Placid Meadows, Pastor Smith is considering two changes. The first would be the addition of a contemporary worship service, which could be offered earlier Sunday morning or even on a Saturday or Sunday evening. The second is to significantly restructure the session and eliminate the current ten committees in favor of ministry teams that would be coordinated by a ministry coordinator but not directed by the session. Pastor Smith has heard about other churches that "released the laity for ministry" and is eager to see if such a restructuring might also release greater energy at Placid Meadows.

Research Findings

At the beginning of the study, I identified four research questions I hoped to answer by the end of the study. Three of the four questions related to my original hypothesis—that a size transition in a congregation would correlate with conflict (a hypothesis not supported by this study). The four essential findings follow.

Finding 1: Most congregations are relatively stable in size— size transitions are uncommon.

Congregations are living organisms nested in dynamic environments, so we should not be surprised that the overwhelming majority in this study reported some significant changes even over a relatively brief (five-year) period. Perhaps the most visible change was among the congregations' leadership—a full 75 percent experienced turnover at some level of full-time paid staff.[21] But programs were also changing, with nearly two-thirds of the congregations adding community-focused programs and more than half initiating programs for current congregational members in the previous five years. During the same period, nearly half of the congregations initiated substantial building projects—ranging from major renovations to complete relocation of the physical plant. In general, however, congregations in this sample remained relatively stable in attendance—only 18 percent experienced an actual size transition during the five-year period studied.

Finding 2: Congregational fights tend to focus on leaders.

Perhaps not surprisingly given all of this change, congregations are also places of conflict. Although slightly less than half of the surveyed congregations (45 percent) reported a major conflict in the previous five years, nearly all the respondents made reference to "significant disagreements" in that same period. Most of the issues reported by respondents from congregations that experienced a conflict fell into one of ten categories:[22]

Leadership (22)
Homosexuality (10)
Personality (8)
Finances (8)
Worship (5)
Power/Control (5)
Theology (5)
Staff (5)

Moral failure (4)
Differing visions (3)

Many congregational leaders believe their congregations are fighting primarily about leadership (including staff other than the lead pastor), theology (including differences over homosexuality), and money. Some experience those disagreements as "personality conflicts," "power struggles," "worship wars," or "differing visions" and occasionally as "moral failure"—but leadership, theology, and resources head the list.

Finding 3: Simply growing or declining does not correlate with conflict.

Surprisingly, there appears to be no significant relationship between size transition (either up or down) and the likelihood of congregational conflict. This means that congregations that crossed a size barrier (such as from family size to pastoral size) were statistically no more likely to experience a conflict than those congregations that did not do so. However, congregations that dramatically declined (that lost 50 or more members during the five-year period) were nearly twice as likely to also have experienced conflict as congregations that were only modestly growing or declining.

Finding 4: Changes to structure and culture highly correlate with conflict.

Either a decision-making change or the addition/deletion of a worship service was often sufficient to precipitate conflict, and a combination of the two events was particularly likely to correlate with conflict. Nine of the 13 congregations that initiated both changes in the five-year period of the study also experienced a major conflict (a rate of nearly 70 percent).

Conflicts about decision making and worship also correspond to two of the four areas reported by Presbyterian congregations participating in the FACT study mentioned in the introduction. The only remaining significant variable from the FACT study not discussed here is conflict over "money/finances/budget." Although only eight respondents explicitly identified finances as a cause of their congregation's conflict, one of the most financially costly of all congregational ventures—building projects—did not correlate at all with conflict.

A congregation's structure and culture both matter. Change in either of these areas significantly correlates with conflict. If the locus or structure of decision making changes, conflict correlates. Worship—the primary expression of a congregation's culture—is the context in which regular attendees experience the congregation's collective energy. If a worship service is added or deleted, conflict correlates. In the next two chapters I discuss these two critical variables at greater length, with the goal of understanding why a change in either of them correlates significantly with congregational conflict. In addition, I address leadership in chapter 4 in an attempt to uncover the extent to which this critical variable might also affect the experience of change and conflict in congregations.

CHAPTER 2

Structure and Power

Every congregation prossesses some form of decision-making structure. Such structures can range from highly centralized, where one person makes all the decisions, to completely decentralized, where everyone participates in all decisions. Rabbi Edwin Friedman viewed these as two extremes on a continuum and suggested that neither "autocratic" leadership nor "consensus" leadership is functional for a congregation.[1] Over time, autocratic leadership disempowers other members and engenders dependency, whereas pure consensus disempowers leadership and can result in a tyranny of the minority. The great majority of congregations occupy some point between these two extremes, usually with a form of representative governance such as an elected lay board.

Structure is important in any organizational system because it formally allocates power and authority. A clear decision-making structure communicates who has the right to make certain decisions. According to organizational scholar David Knoke, "The fundamental issue in organizational governance is the distribution and legitimation of power among a collectivity's participants."[2] Thus, structure acts to confer legitimacy on those individuals who are granted authority within the system. As the great German sociologist Max Weber observed, "Authority is legitimized power."[3] And power that is seen as legitimately conferred is less likely to be contested.

Thus, a clear and clearly communicated decision-making structure functions to reduce destructive conflict in a congregation. Many power struggles within a congregation are fights over who has the right to exercise authority in a given situation. Can a particular lay leader make this decision, or does she need to consult with church staff first? Is this a matter that the pastor and staff can handle, or does the board need to be involved? Does the board have the right to resolve this issue, or does it need to be brought to the entire congregation? A clear and clearly communicated structure—including up-to-date bylaws and a posted organizational chart—will offer guidelines about where decision-making authority should be lodged.

A decision-making structure has a second function related to power. Not only does structure allocate authority, it also indicates lines of accountability and limits to the authority that is granted. In other words, a healthy structure both confers power and limits its exercise. The basic distinction between "executive authority" (granted to staff) and "legislative authority" (granted to the board) is an effort to ensure a balance of power between clergy and lay members. Following the bylaws may seem tedious and time consuming, but the bylaws exist in part to protect the congregation and its members from the unchecked abuse of power by individual members. If bylaws are changed, and sometimes they need to be, the process should encourage careful reflection and invite broad participation.

Since structure is so important to the health and functioning of a congregation, it is not surprising that efforts to change a congregation's structure might be fraught with conflict. Structure allocates power; so when we mess with power arrangements, we should expect conflict. Let's consider each of the structural variables mentioned in the introduction—decision-making structure, physical structure, size, and age—to see if changes to any of them actually correlated with conflict in this study.

Size Transitions and Structure Change

Size is a significant structural variable, and there is little debate that congregations need to adjust their decision-making structures as they grow. In family-size congregations, the "church boss" (a long-tenured lay member or family) tends to make the major decisions; in pastoral-size congregations, the pastor and board often decide together; and in program-size congregations, the board and church staff make key decisions. By the time a congregation is corporate- or mega-sized, decision making often reverts to the lead pastor—albeit with delegated authority to key staff and a board that sets policy and reviews major decisions. Put simply, family-size congregations are usually lay led, corporate and larger churches are clergy led, and pastoral- and program-size congregations tend to be jointly led.

The size transitions literature suggests congregations that fail to adjust their decision-making structures after a size transition are at a greater risk of conflict. Former Alban Institute senior consultant Roy Pneuman cites as one of nine causes of congregational conflict that "the structure no longer fits the congregation's size."[4] Alice Mann, currently an Alban Institute senior consultant, notes that failure to add staff as a congregation gets larger can inhibit healthy growth.[5] Finally, congregations that successfully changed, sociologist Nancy Ammerman observes, "have also had to work hard at creating and recreating their decision-making structures."[6]

As important as changing decision-making structure might be, does the failure to change structure after a size transition really correlate with conflict? While 9 of the 18 congregations in the study that underwent a size transition also experienced conflict (a rate of 50 percent), 35 of the 79 congregations that did not experience a size transition also experienced conflict (44 percent), a rate nearly identical to the conflict rate of the overall sample (45 percent). This suggests that the simple process of going through a size transition does indeed increase, albeit only slightly, a congregation's likelihood of experiencing a conflict.

Can this slight increase in conflict likelihood be attributed to failure to change the decision-making structure after a size transition? The research in this study found a significant correlation not between size transitions and conflict but between *changes in decision-making structure* and conflict. In only 6 of the 36 congregations that reported changes to decision-making structure did the conflict precede the change to the decision-making structure. This suggests that in only a small minority of the cases the structural changes came in response to the conflict. Of the 30 remaining cases, 19 of the congregations reported a conflict the same year as or subsequent to the reported change to decision-making structure. This means that nearly two-thirds of congregations that changed their structure also experienced a concurrent or subsequent conflict.

Also, among those 30 remaining cases, 16 (more than half) occurred in pastoral-size congregations. This implies that pastoral-size congregations are by far the likeliest venue for changes in decision-making structure and is consistent with the claim that transitioning from a pastoral-size to a program-size congregation is generally the toughest of the size transitions.[7] Leaders of pastoral-size congregations often seem to be aware that they need to change the structure and culture of their congregations if they are to successfully overcome the 200 barrier. Therefore, it is logical that pastoral-size congregations are responsible for the majority of the structure-change cases.

Because I requested both the year of the conflict and the year of the change in decision-making structure, causal directions are possible to establish. A three-way cross-tabulation confirms it was not congregations that *failed* to change their structure that were most likely to experience conflict, but rather the ones that *did* change their structures. Of the six congregations that underwent a size transition *and* changed their decision-making struc-

Figure 2.1. Size transitions, structure changes, and conflict.

18 18% of total sample	Total number of congregations that experienced a size transition
9 50% of total transition cases	Congregations that experienced *a size transition and experienced conflict*
5 55% of transition and conflict cases	Congregations that experienced *a size transition, changed structure, and experienced a conflict*
4 45% of transition and conflict cases	Congregations that experienced *a size transition and changed structure but did not experience a conflict*

ture, two did not experience conflict and four did. Although this is a very small sample, it indicates that even for congregations undergoing size transitions, a change to their decision-making structure is more likely to *invite* conflict than to deter it. Congregations may be well advised to change their structures after undergoing a size transition, but the reason for doing so should not be to avert a conflict. In fact, they should probably anticipate one.

Physical structure is yet another area where change might introduce conflict. For a congregation, physical structure regards the external footprint of buildings and the internal layout of offices, worship space, and classrooms. While physical structure is often considered to be as important as the social structure (formal and informal relationships) for an organization, this study found only a slight correlation between building projects and conflict. While 46 of the congregations in the study undertook a building project during the five-year period studied, they experienced conflict at only a slightly higher rate than the general population of congregations.[8] I will explore this phenomenon in chapter 5, which addresses change and conflict, as I believe there is much we can learn from the relative success at conducting building projects in ways that do not precipitate destructive conflict.

The final structural variable mentioned earlier is the age of a congregation and particularly its point on the lifecycle curve. Seminary professor and congregational consultant Israel Galindo, author of *The Hidden Lives of Congregations*, argues that differing leadership styles are needed in each of eight lifespan stages of a congregation. These leadership functions also have implications for the kind of decision-making structure a congregation needs as it is established, grows, and matures. In my experience, congregations in the three latter stages of Galindo's model (maturity, aristocracy, and bureaucracy) will be the most likely to resist significant structural changes.[9] The more mature a congregation and the stronger its homeostasis, the more likely it will be to resist structural changes.[10]

From Committees to Teams

What prompts a congregation to change its decision-making structure? In this study of congregations, many of the respondents who described a change in decision-making structure did so in terms of a transition from committees to teams. Respondents who addressed this issue often described a desire to "push decision-making power down" and to encourage decision making by "empowered teams" rather than by committees of the board. In practical terms, roles were changing from committee chairs typically appointed by the governing body to team leaders who were often selected by the teams themselves. Consider this example, drawn from a composite of cases of congregations that have undergone structure change processes:

> First Downtown Church is located in a mature neighborhood of a major city in the southwestern United States. Established nearly one hundred years ago, the congregation has seen its environment change significantly over the past fifty years

and is now located in a mixed community of expensive downtown lofts and extensive homelessness. First Downtown is proud of its history and its ongoing service to the community. Nearly a dozen ministries—serving the poor, homeless, and immigrant populations—operate from the premises of First Downtown. A number of these ministries were started by volunteers from First Downtown, but many are now independent nonprofit organizations.

Rev. Johnson came to First Downtown about ten years ago and is widely appreciated for her pastoral ministry and effective teaching and preaching. She is seen as a strong advocate for lay ministry in the community and the parish and has encouraged the start-up of five or six new ministries in the past ten years alone. Attendance has also rebounded during Rev. Johnson's tenure, reversing a long period of decline that started in the 1980s.

But Rev. Johnson has been increasingly frustrated with the slow pace of change in the congregation itself and what she views as the resistance within the vestry to truly becoming a church of the community—not just for the community. Many of the newer members live in the area surrounding First Downtown but are not significantly included in the decision-making structures of the parish. Several of these newer members serve on church committees that minister in the local community, but have confided that they feel controlled and demeaned by the vestry members who head their committees.

Last year Rev. Johnson attended a workshop, "Releasing Your Church for Ministry," and was inspired by the possibilities of transforming the many committees in the congregation to ministry teams. Instead of bureaucratic committees chaired by vestry members, Rev. Johnson would like to see ministry teams led by passionate laypeople under the leadership of a ministry coordinator—not controlled by the vestry.

Rev. Johnson introduced the idea of moving from committees to teams at the last vestry meeting. There were some questions about the implications, but Rev. Johnson promised that she would give at least six months to a year for the transition, and that seemed to ease concerns. Several vestry members seemed very excited about the possibilities and several others sounded concerned, while most appeared noncommittal about the proposal. Nonetheless, the proposal passed with a voice vote.

After getting approval from the vestry, Rev. Johnson prepared an announcement for the congregation regarding the proposed transition. In the written announcement, she stressed that moving from committees to teams would "release people for ministry" and that it would also free the vestry to focus on spiritual leadership of the parish rather than administrative oversight of the many current committees.

Within an hour, Rev. Johnson was receiving negative responses in her e-mail in-box. Several of the committee chairs seemed particularly concerned. What about accountability? Who would provide the necessary oversight? Who would approve the budgets of these various teams? Rev. Johnson suspected that some of the opposition was due to the reality that once the team model was implemented, current committee chairs would no longer have the power they currently enjoyed.

At the next vestry meeting the tone was considerably different from the previous month. Several of the previously concerned vestry members were now clearly opposed to the proposal and questioned why Rev. Johnson was pushing this initiative as strongly as she was. One even asked if it wasn't time for Rev. Johnson to consider whether this parish was where she was still called to serve. Convinced that the shift to ministry teams was still the right direction to go, Rev. Johnson proposed that a task force be established to study how to most effectively make the transition and report back to the vestry within three months.

This story illustrates several key points regarding changes to structure and subsequent conflict. First, pressures resulting from growth as well as a simple desire for growth often motivate efforts to restructure. Second, a decision-making structure that seems quite adequate to the majority in an organization or a community may be quite unsatisfactory to a significant minority. (The story of the disgruntled Greek-speaking believers in Acts 6 also illustrates this reality.) Third, proposed changes to an existing decision-making structure often precipitate conflict and anxiety. Finally, the ability of leadership to stay nonanxious and connected to others in the system is the primary determinant of the system's ability to weather a restructuring crisis and emerge healthier.

As noted, one of the most common structural changes reported by respondents to the congregational survey was a shift from a committee model of decision making to a team model. In the team model, authority for decision making is shifted from committees reporting to a board to semiautonomous teams that are often more loosely tied to the governance structure. Aside from the messiness of the transition from committees to teams, there can also be a genuine loss of power for committee chairs, who often have also served as members of the governing board (the session or vestry).

Congregations experience pressure from their institutional environments to adopt team-based ministry. Christian websites and books tout teams as both biblical and more effective. Committees are described as fitting an "institutional" way of doing church, while teams belong to "a mission-driven mindset." It is unlikely that these authors realize that their institutional metaphors have simply shifted from those used in the organizational hierarchy model that prevailed from the 1950s through the 1970s to ones that match the current emphasis on decentralized teams adopted from business models that emerged in the 1980s and 1990s.

In *Business without Bosses: How Self-Managing Teams Are Building High-Performance Companies*, authors Charles Manz and Henry Sims urged corporate leaders to adopt the team-based model of decentralized decision making.[11] Propelled by the financial pressure to reduce middle management layers, the model spread throughout corporate America with varying degrees of success. What corporate America has adopted over the past twenty years has affected the religious sector in the past decade. Whether this is a positive development seems to vary by congregation. Some congregations have made the transition from committees to teams effectively, whereas others have not. As one pastor who had led transitions from committees to teams in two congregations commented, "The way the change is done seems to matter even more than the change itself."

Power and Structure

What are the mechanisms that explain the relationship between structural changes and conflict, and how might this phenomenon work in congregations? Of the 100 pastors interviewed for the study underlying this book, 43 offered comments regarding structure that I was able to record during the phone interviews. Several of these directly addressed the issue of power in structure change, including the following:

- "Power used to lie in the pastor, and the session would go along, but we're moving to a team model with the pastor as coach."
- "When I came, the power lay totally in the session. We're trying to move the power downward."

• "The real power lies with the congregation. If you don't bring them on board, they vote with their pocketbooks."

Note that power is described as residing at three different places in these examples—with the pastor, with the session, and with the congregation—despite the fact that all three congregations are program sized. The first two pastors whose comments are recorded above also undertook changes to the decision-making structures of their congregations. Yet neither leader reported a congregational conflict during the five-year reporting period, despite the fact that about 70 percent (25 of 36) of the congregations that reported a change to decision making also reported a conflict.[12]

Could it be that leaders who are more aware of the underlying power dynamics in a system are less likely to precipitate destructive conflict dynamics when they initiate changes to decision-making structure? It is not possible to draw any firm conclusions from this modest sample. However, the fact that the two pastors who directly addressed power issues during their interviews headed congregations that were an exception to the general rule (that a change to decision making correlates with conflict) suggests that this question merits further examination.

In nonreligious organizations, power is a more visible currency. Organizational sociologist Rosabeth Kanter observes that power is a function not only of one's position in the structural hierarchy but also of competence, "a neglected side of power."[13] Kanter adds that structural reorganizations are seldom undertaken to improve organizational effectiveness, but rather are often a "way to manipulate the structure to increase power."[14] Kanter also suggests that even those in designated positions of organizational authority might have very circumscribed power. Authority without power tends to produce controlling and coercive bosses. At the industrial company she studied, Kanter observed "relatively powerless managers who were insecure about their organizational status tended to give the least freedom to subordinates and to personally control their department's activities much more tightly."[15] By establishing a link between insecurity and authoritarianism, Kanter is also implicitly suggesting a connection between security and empowerment.

Organizational development specialists Larry Greiner and Virginia Schein underline the importance of understanding power dynamics in organizations as well as the reality of political behaviors. "The key to understanding power in organizations is to acknowledge the pervasive reality of political behavior across and throughout all organizational forms. It means accepting power as natural and necessary to decision making regardless of formal structure."[16]

Congregations are a subset of organizations and are therefore the locus of political and power dynamics, as are other organizations. However, congregational leaders appear less likely than other organizational leaders to acknowledge their own power and the power of their organizations. This reluctance may be due to the desire on the part of many pastors to be seen as servants of Christ and of the people in the congregation. Yet, this failure to acknowledge power has been described as one of the roots of clergy sexual abuse, as some pastors seem unable to accept that their role creates a situation of unequal power vis-à-vis parishioners or counselees.[17] Discomfort with power, and the accompanying inability to deal openly with renegotiation of power relationships inherent in any structural change, may also be one of the factors driving the correlation between conflict and changes to decision-making structure in congregations.

In addition to the denial of power mechanism, I would offer a second possible explanation for the correlation between structural changes and conflict. In my twenty years as an organizational consultant, I have observed that the process of changing a structure (what organizations call restructuring) tends to surface existing but latent interpersonal conflicts and power imbalances. The issue is not just "who gets the corner office" but also whose role will be enhanced and whose diminished in the proposed restructure. The mere process of discussing such changes tends to unleash significant anxiety in an organizational system, and the anxiety itself may propel the underlying conflict dynamics to the surface. This was seen in the earlier example of First Downtown Church.

Structure and Authority in the Bible

The Bible has only a few examples of organizational restructuring. In the Old Testament the children of Israel transitioned from leadership by prophets to leadership by kings—one of the earliest recorded examples of mimetic isomorphism.[18] In the New Testament, the earliest church in Jerusalem had to create a new structural role (that of deacon) to deal with a conflict over care given to the widows of its Greek-speaking minority. This structural innovation allowed the apostles to continue to work within their job description ("prayer and the ministry of the word") while the system also attended to the physical needs of the widows.[19]

The apostle Paul, considered by many scholars to be the founder of Christianity, attended to structure as he established congregations throughout the Roman world. In his letters to both Timothy and Titus, Paul lists qualifications for overseers (elders) and deacons, noting that how a potential leader manages his or her family should be a criterion for selection to a church leadership role. It appears that Paul modeled the structure of these early and scattered congregations on the first church in Jerusalem—elders appointed for spiritual leadership and deacons to care for physical needs.

Paul also found that his own authority as an apostle was contested, and he responded vigorously to those who questioned his right to claim apostleship. Paul began many of his letters with the greeting, "Paul, an apostle . . ." and often referred to his unique encounter with Christ on the road to Damascus and subsequent confirmation of his calling by the apostles in Jerusalem. Paul was forced to assert his calling and authority because he was neither one of the original twelve apostles nor installed in a church office that would have conferred legitimacy. As a movement rather than an organization, the early church had only two designated leadership roles—apostles and deacons—and the process to become an apostle after Jesus's death and resurrection was not entirely clear.

But while leadership contests (including between Peter and Paul, as recorded in Galatians 2) are often present, structure per se does not appear to be a major cause of conflict in the New Testament.[20] The books that comprise our New Testament are a record of Christianity's earliest days. Not until the book of Revelation do we encounter more mature congregations, and these congregations are praised or condemned for their passion for God's kingdom and for their internal morality—not for their decision-making structures. Structure is an organizational reality, not a biblical imperative. Yet it is a reality that demands the attention of organizational leaders, as structure can inhibit organizational growth when it does not adapt to change and can spark conflict when it is changed without careful attention to the implications.

Some Conclusions about Structure and Power

Combining the above discussion with the empirical findings from the congregational study, I offer the following conclusions.

- The failure to adapt a congregation's structure when it is growing can inhibit growth (a claim consistent with both Alice Mann's and Nancy Ammerman's findings).
- The failure to clarify a congregation's decision-making structure, including roles and responsibilities, will tend to

produce destructive power struggles between formal and informal leaders who are contesting unclear roles.

- A change in a congregation's structure is by definition a realignment of the power relationships within the congregation, as structure allocates power.
- Changes to a congregation's decision-making structure correlate with conflict and also appear to have a causal relationship with conflict.
- Conflict may result not only when some members resist the changing power dynamics, but also when the change in structure surfaces latent conflict in the system. When the infrastructure of any system is rattled, the cobwebs of conflict are likely to also be shaken loose.
- Congregational leaders who are aware of these dynamics may be more capable of preparing their systems to deal with the resistance and conflict that are likely to result from attempts to change the congregation's structure.

Congregations that fail to adapt their decision-making structures are also likely to fail to grow. But when congregations do adjust their decision-making structures, conflict is likely to result. I have suggested that changing power dynamics and the surfacing of latent conflicts are two possible explanations for this phenomenon. In the following chapter I address the correlation between conflict and changes to worship and also consider the mechanisms by which the addition of or a change to a worship service might precipitate conflict in a congregation.

CHAPTER 3

Worship—the Primary Expression of a Congregation's Culture

Worship is the central act of virtually every congregation in the United States. All recent major studies of congregations have affirmed this claim, as does the weekly experience of those who attend congregations. Sociologist of religion Mark Chaves lists worship events, religious education, and artistic production as the "core activities" among congregations participating in the 1998 National Congregations Study (NCS).[1] Congregational researcher Nancy Ammerman observes that the "single most common congregational activity is a weekly worship event," while Penny Edgell cites worship and religious education as the two functions consistently emphasized in all four of the congregational models she found among 23 congregations studied in the Chicago area.[2]

Many of the survey respondents in my study emphasized the central position of worship in their congregations. As one respondent commented, "The congregation was traditionally organized almost entirely around the worship experience." Others linked adding a worship service to a deliberate effort at outreach, noting that worship was the primary way newcomers first encountered the congregation. One respondent praised his congregation's "willingness to try something with contemporary worship (on a weekday evening) to reach a new segment of the community."

The claim that worship is the primary focus of congregations will find little debate. Further, the worship event itself possesses several remarkably common elements despite the range of worship styles and expressions. The Faith Communities Today (FACT) study found that a sermon and music characterized nearly every worship service.[3] Likewise, the National Congregations Study (NCS) study concluded that a sermon (or speech) and congregational singing are "essentially universal" elements in the worship service.[4]

Yet the content and style of that sermon and singing have produced an impressive variety of worship modalities—as well as conflict among advocates of particular forms of worship. On their surface, the arguments appear to be about differing styles—particularly styles of musical expression. Books regarding "worship wars" written for congregational practitioners claim that this conflict is based on underlying anxiety over changing cultural and demographic patterns within mainline congregations.[5] The proposed solution is to transcend the traditional versus contemporary dichotomy and offer worship that is truly "blended."

But preferences for different styles alone offer a thin explanation for the persistence and virulence of these worship wars in congregations. Of the 100 congregations I studied, 42 reported a significant change in worship in the previous five years—defined as adding or eliminating a worship service. Thirty-three of these congregations added a worship service, five dropped a service, and four both added and dropped a service during the period studied. Nearly two-thirds of congregations that reported a significant change in worship during the period of study (26 of 42) also reported at least one significant conflict event. Controlling for variables such as polity, age, size, and pastoral tenure, adding or dropping a service increased the odds of experiencing a conflict by 3.3 times.[6] Unfortunately, it is not possible to establish the causal direction on the basis of this study alone, as the precise year of the worship change was not requested during the interviews.

Many of the nine worship services that were dropped were likely discontinued in response to a congregational conflict and declining numbers.[7] Yet there is also a notable correlation between the mere addition of a worship service—often described by respondents as "contemporary"—and an experience of congregational conflict. Of the 36 congregations that reported adding a worship service, 21 (58 percent) also reported experiencing a conflict during the five-year period of the study. This compares to 24 of 61 congregations (39 percent) that did not add a worship service but still experienced conflict.

Adding a worship service also correlates with church size, as larger congregations are more likely to be growing and are generally more capable of adding a service. While only about a quarter of the family- and pastoral-size congregations (16 of 65) added a service in the five-year reporting period, nearly 60 percent of the program- and corporate-size congregations reported doing

Figure 3.1. Worship changes and conflict. Sample size: 100 congregations.

42 (42%)	Number and percent of congregations that *added and/or deleted* a worship service
26 (62%)	Number and percent of these congregations that *also experienced a conflict*
36 (36%)	Number and percent of congregations that *added* a worship service
21 (58%)	Number and percent of congregations *adding a worship service that also experienced a conflict*
61 (61%)	Number and percent of congregations that did not add a worship service
24 (39%)	Number and percent of congregations that did not add a worship service but experienced conflict

so (20 of 35). But regardless of size category, adding a worship service correlated with increased likelihood of conflict.

These results support the hypothesis that congregations of any size that add a worship service are at greater risk of conflict than those that do not add a service. But will adding a worship service also produce church growth? Fifty-three percent of congregations that added a worship service also demonstrated numerical growth over the five-year period. Because in the entire study only 44 percent of the 100 congregations reported numerical growth, it does appear that adding a worship service may correlate modestly with growth. But there is only limited support for the premise that adding a worship service will necessarily lead to church growth. Adding a service is even more likely, apparently, to lead to conflict.

Given the risks, why might an established congregation with an apparently well-functioning traditional worship service choose to disrupt homeostasis by adding a second or third worship service? In many cases respondents volunteered that the new worship service was a "contemporary" worship service. Several motivations are possible, including the following.

First, congregations exist in a competitive marketplace, and both organizational sociology and management theory suggest that the successful ones will make adaptive efforts to respond to changes in that environment. If the worship preferences of an older generation are no longer shared by younger or newer members and attendance begins to suffer, a change in worship style might be predicted to follow. As one pastor who responded to my survey remarked, "New members wanted a broadening of the music program." Another frustrated respondent who was advocating a contemporary service lamented, "The community has changed, but the congregation has not."

Second, congregations also operate in institutional fields and are influenced by successful models from sister congregations. When the megachurch on the other side of town begins to offer contemporary worship with a variety of bands and live video feeds, the pressure on smaller congregations to do likewise can become significant.

Finally, cultural anthropologist Margaret Mead suggested that Americans tend to become "bored with repetition," and this tendency could also explain the decline of traditional rituals in some congregations.[8] As one Episcopal respondent noted, "Seven years ago we were isolated, using the 1928 prayer book. Now our average age is 37 . . . and we have four services on a Sunday!"

In sum, congregational leaders might make changes to their worship services to attract nonmembers, to attempt to keep up with the Willow Creeks, or simply to alleviate the boredom of current members.[9] Regardless of the motivation for such a change, however, the result is likely to be that some members are pleased with the changes while others are displeased. Members and leaders who advocated the change to a more contemporary service are likely to be supportive, while those who resisted the innovation are likely to question its existence and even to boycott the new service.[10] An illustration adapted from one of the participating congregations in the study may illuminate the challenges involved in adding a contemporary service.

> For the past thirty years, Casa Vieja Congregation offered a single traditional worship service every Sunday during the summer and two identical services during the winter months, when winter visitors would flood into the desert. In the mid-1990s, however, key lay leaders in the congregation began to advocate adding a contemporary service that would have more appeal to younger attendees. After some wrangling in the church board, especially over the right time for this service, the new service was launched at the key 11:00 hour, with the traditional service scheduled at 9:00 a.m.
>
> The initial rumblings from older members focused primarily on logistics. Rather than choosing to come at either

9:00 or 11:00 for a traditional worship service, they now could come only at 9:00—unless they wanted to hear the "awful music" accompanying the new contemporary service. But a second theme was heard from members of both groups. While the older members attending at 9:00 complained there were no young people in their worship service, some of the younger families attending at 11:00 noted that they missed the "salt-and-pepper heads" that had previously been sprinkled throughout the sanctuary.

Within a year of the implementation of the contemporary service, the congregation had effectively divided into two congregations. The 9:00 service consisted primarily of members born prior to 1950, while the 11:00 service consisted primarily of baby boomers and their children. Interestingly, the implementation of a second contemporary service did not produce a spike in overall worship attendance. And beyond the periodic griping about worship times and bemoaning that the church had splintered by generation, there was little overt conflict over the addition of a contemporary worship service.

Significant conflict did arise within the board, however, about two years after the implementation of the new worship service. The conflict was framed primarily as differing visions for the future of the congregation, with the pastor and some of his supporters arguing for a stronger emphasis on evangelism and outreach, while other lay leaders, who had earlier advocated adding the contemporary service, urging a greater focus on worship and Christian education.

As noted, congregations that reported a significant change to their worship services experienced conflict at about a 50 percent higher rate than congregations that did not.[11] Controlling for key demographic variables such as the age and size of the congregation, the odds of experiencing a conflict increased by approximately 3.3 times when a new worship service was added.

Congregations that adapt their worship practices—especially by adding a new worship service—are indeed at a higher risk of conflict. But congregations that fail to adapt to a changing environment may be at much greater risk. Based on her research, Penny Edgell concludes that they are "not likely to survive past the life spans of their current members."[12]

Why might adding a worship service correlate with a significantly higher rate of conflict?[13] Two possible reasons appear in the congregational studies literature.

Disruption of Ritual

The first hypothesis suggests that when a new worship service is added—or an existing service significantly transformed—the congregation's central method of meaning making is greatly affected. As Chaves writes, "Congregations' central purpose is of course the expression and transmission of religious meaning, and corporate worship is the primary way in which that purpose is pursued."[14] Chaves also charts the sociologically well-known process of "routinization of charisma," by which worship practices tend over time to become less enthusiastic and more ceremonial.[15] Established congregations in the Presbyterian and Episcopal tradition, even in the fast growing and relatively new state of Arizona, are likely to be well along the routinization of charisma continuum that sociologist Max Weber first described. Nested in dynamic environments with changing demographics, however, such congregations may also find themselves innovating with more emotionally expressive services designed to appeal to a younger audience.[16]

But the change to the rituals and artifacts of the worship service may signal to congregants that deeper level cultural changes are underway. A congregation that transitions from using an established denominational hymnbook to singing "off the wall" praise music projected onto a screen may be unintentionally provoking troubling questions in some adherents, questions such as:

- What does this transition signal about our loyalty to the denomination and our future as a true Presbyterian/ Episcopal church?
- How will our young people learn the core tenets of our faith if they are singing praise music rather than the more theologically grounded hymns of the past?

According to Edgar Schein's typology of organizational culture, visible rituals and artifacts represent the tip of the iceberg of an organization's culture. Congregational rituals include not only obvious ritualized celebrations such as communion, but also acts like congregational singing that over time will become a ritualized process. Artifacts in a congregation include musical instruments such as an organ and piano. When, for example, the organ is replaced by a drum set, a significant change of artifacts has occurred.

Visible rituals and artifacts are supported by additional levels of congregational culture. At the middle level are values and norms that can often be articulated by the organization's members and are expressed in the visible artifacts and rituals. But at the base of the iceberg are the unwritten and invisible beliefs and assumptions that support the top two layers.

When rituals and artifacts are transformed, organization members might understandably wonder if the congregation's underlying values and norms are also negotiable. And any threat to conscious values and norms will threaten the largely unconscious beliefs and assumptions. Worship wars, from such an organizational-cultural perspective, are quite understandable. When the primary meaning-making device—the worship service—is negotiable, congregants may conclude that the ground underneath may be shifting as well.

To understand the role of worship in a religious community, we must also examine the role of ritual and symbol in that community's life. Eastern Mennonite University Professor of Peacebuilding Lisa Schirch writes that ritual "uses symbolic actions to communicate a forming or transforming message in a unique social space."[17] "Symbolic actions" for Schirch include rituals. She describes forming rituals as those that reinforce the status quo by forming people's worldviews, identities, and relationships, whereas transforming rituals "mark and assist in the process of change."

Applying this typology to traditional and contemporary worship experiences, it is likely that many in a congregation will have experienced the worship ritual as a forming experience that they value in part for its socializing function for their children and grandchildren. When this ritual instead assumes a transforming function and becomes a marker of change within the congregation, conflict might result. Even if underlying values and beliefs are not being fundamentally challenged, the fear that such transformation may occur could be pervasive.

Ritual provides security as well as meaning. As dramatist Eric Bertish suggests, "Ritual is important because it imposes order on what would otherwise be an uncontrollable existence. Certain things must be done, no matter the circumstance, because in so doing I gain control of my life, if only for those few moments. This control is vital to my sense of well being for without it the universe has prevailed and overwhelmed me."[18]

Despite the dramatic flourish, Bertish may be on to a significant insight: *ritual imposes order on what would otherwise be an uncontrollable existence.* Some may attend worship not only to obtain meaning but also to obtain control, if only for an hour. When contemporary worship is introduced and familiar mechanisms for meaning and control are disrupted, conflict might logically follow.

Given that conflict over music styles seems to be at the heart of many worship wars, we also might ask what is so significant about congregational music in worship. Mark Chaves addresses this in his comprehensive study of U.S. congregations. Music is the most pervasive element of worship, included in the worship services of 96 percent of congregations in the NCS study—slightly ahead even of the sermon or speech that is part of 95 percent of congregations' worship. And the worship service experienced by the average attendee in the NCS study included both twenty minutes of music and twenty minutes of a sermon. While worship is what matters most to congregations, music and the sermon are clearly the two most important elements.

Perhaps the change of musical styles implied in a shift to contemporary worship is unsettling to congregants for one of four reasons. The first is simple familiarity. Long-term members know what to do when instructed to "turn to hymn number 209 and sing the first, third, and fifth stanzas," but they may not feel as comfortable when asked to "join hands and sing with all your heart" the latest praise song. The second possible reason involves the disruption of ritual that occurs when congregants are asked to look at the projected words on a screen rather than to look down at the hymnals in their hands. A third possibility is that some members may genuinely object to what they view as the simplistic theology of some newer praise music. Finally, some members may simply find the guitars and drums that tend to be part of most praise bands to be loud and annoying.

Mennonite pastor and writer Shane Hipps revisits Marshall McLuhan's seminal work to explore another consideration, the "hidden power of electronic culture" in the church. Recounting communications writer Marshall McLuhan's familiar dictum that "the medium is the message," Hipps contrasts the "individualizing" role of the printing press in the modernist period with the "retribalizing" influence of electronic media in the current postmodern period. Hipps describes current electronic culture as creating a "tribe of individuals" who through the electronic media "develop a new appreciation for mystery, experience and intuition as central elements of faith."[19] These "electronic tribes" are connected through social networking sites on the Internet but also come to church expecting connection.

Since for Rev. Hipps the "left brain tyranny" of the modern era produced linear and sequential thinking that privileged objectivity and rationality, there is potential for a clash of worldviews between the modernist and postmodernist approaches to worship. While the former individualizes the worship experience with private hymnals and a linear order of worship, the latter tribalizes it through group singing and sometimes-unpredictable mystical experiences. Although these tribal experiences may not be electronically mediated in a corporate worship experience, participants in worship have been shaped by electronic and Internet culture. Conflict would seem logical between advocates of a linear, logical, and individual approach to worship and those who desire mystical, experiential, and corporate worship.

Particularly interesting is Hipps's hypothesis that the changing societal environment—especially evidenced by the rapid diffusion of electronic media in congregations—may be fueling a clash of worldviews that propels the worship wars. In this view, the Episcopal Church's 1928 Book of Common Prayer is not only an artifact of a particular belief system but also a proxy for an individualistic, linear, and rational worldview. The abandonment of the Prayer Book in favor of a PowerPoint projection of words and images thus introduces a competing postmodern worldview that is collective, mystical, and intuitive. When worldviews clash, conflict is all but inevitable.

Disruption of Group Cohesion

In addition to this "disruption of ritual" hypothesis to explain conflict over changes to worship, a second hypothesis relates to the congregation's function as a social entity. According to the size transitions literature, family- or pastoral-size congregations are single-cell organisms. In other words, they function both in worship services and in social gatherings as single groups that gather all active members at a particular time and place. As Alban senior consultant Alice Mann explains: "Congregations of these two sizes tend to be relatively homogeneous in makeup. Each revolves around a central relationship that can be immediately and intuitively apprehended: the relationship among members as a 'primary group' or 'single cell' (family-size church) or the dyadic relationship between the sole ordained leader and the congregation (pastoral-size church). The congregation's identity is largely inherent in these central relationships."[20]

When a second worship service is introduced into this context, the social integrity of the group is threatened, and conflict might logically ensue. While the goal of the worship organizers might be to "welcome newcomers to our church," the perception of established members could easily be that the social bonds are being severed.

But the research reviewed in this book did not find a higher level of conflict over worship among single-cell congregations than among multiple-cell program- and corporate-size congregations. While 9 of the 16 family- and pastoral-size congregations that added a worship service experienced a conflict (a 56 percent rate), 7 of the 16 did not experience conflict (44 percent)—a proportion consistent with the overall conflict experience of congregations that added worship services. Indeed, these percentages are actually closer together than the 60 percent of program- and corporate-size congregations that added a worship service and experienced conflict (12 of 20) compared to the 40 percent that added a service and did not (8 of 20).

The "disruption of homeostasis" that, according to family systems theory, is caused by significant change may offer an explanation for these conflicts regardless of the size of the congregation. But the congregational-size explanation that links disruption of a single-cell organism via the introduction of a second service to congregational conflict is not supported by this research. Both small and large congregations are more likely to experience conflict if they add a worship service than if they do not, and they are likely to do so at approximately the same rate.

Conflict over Worship in Corinth

In his first letter to Corinthian believers, Paul responds to concerns over the conduct of worship in Corinth. There apparently was significant conflict in the church in Corinth over how to properly worship—particularly focused on the use of tongues and prophesying during worship. Paul's comments in chapters 12 through 14 make it clear that he is concerned about the impact on other members of these various gifts and about "good order in worship."[21] Paul concludes that he wants the Corinthians to permit speaking in tongues and to encourage prophesying, but to do everything "in a fitting and orderly way" (1 Cor. 14:40).

Figure 3.2. Church size and changes to worship.

20 (57%)	Number and percent of congregations *over 200 that added a service*
12 (60%)	Number and percent of these congregations that *also experienced conflict*
16 (25%)	Number and percent of congregations *under 200 that added a service*
9 (56%)	Number and percent of these congregations *that also experienced conflict*

Sample size: 100 congregations
35 congregations over 200 worship attendance
65 congregations 200 or fewer worship attendance

Throughout his comments on worship and the expression of various gifts in worship, Paul seems primarily concerned about the attitude that the Corinthian believers bring to worship. Whatever spiritual gifts individuals possess, Paul is most concerned that they are filled with love. "Love is patient, love is kind. It does not envy, it does not boast, it is not proud," Paul writes. He continues, "Love never fails. But where there are prophecies, they will cease; where there are tongues, they will be stilled; where there is knowledge, it will pass away" (1 Cor. 13:4, 8).

Paul's two principles regarding worship thus deal with order and attitude. Paul is quite willing to see a variety of worship expressions but wants them offered within an orderly framework. And he is willing to welcome the range of gifts that individuals bring to worship (including speaking in tongues, prophesying, and interpretation) but reminds everyone that the greatest gift is love (13:13). Perhaps for Paul good order is itself an expression of love—recognition that for many members feeling out of control threatens their entire experience of worship. Paul's overriding concern seems to be the health of the body—what builds up the church rather than elevating particular individuals.

If we apply these principles to our modern worship wars, we might develop an ethic that values a variety of worship expressions within a context of order and love. An orderly structure to worship reduces the threat that a disruption of ritual poses to those who treasure tradition and familiar ritual. And an attitude of love makes it less likely that the introduction of a new service will split the congregation into two ever-more-distant groups.

In conclusion, changes to worship (defined as adding or deleting a worship service) correlate with conflict. Correlation is not causation, but a qualitative assessment of respondents' comments suggests that the inauguration of a contemporary service often does precede a conflict episode.[22] We have explored two possible explanatory mechanisms for this relationship, a disruption of ritual and a disruption of group cohesion.

The former thesis is strongly supported by this study while the latter is less so.[23]

And from the 1 Corinthians passage on worship, we learn that the principles of orderliness and love may reduce the likelihood of destructive conflict in response to innovations in worship. Clear structure is our friend when it comes to both decision making and worship services. And an attitude of love covers a multitude of mistakes when beginning or revising a worship service. Conducting worship or making changes to a service "lovingly and in order" may be the most efficient paraphrase of Paul's guidelines. In chapter 6, the concluding chapter, I offer additional suggestions for introducing changes to worship in ways that are less likely to produce destructive conflict.

CHAPTER 4

Leadership in Congregations

We have reviewed both structural (decision-making) and cultural (worship) implications from the research, noting significant correlations between conflict and a change to either area in congregations. We will now consider what is often thought to be the most important variable in congregational life—leadership. The research found a significant correlation between congregational conflict and leadership turnover, which we will explore in this chapter.

Leadership matters. Successful organizations often revere a current or past leader who was particularly effective at organization building. Founding leaders may take on mythic qualities—such as Dr. Bob Pierce, the founder of World Vision. World Vision employees commonly repeat and are clearly still inspired by Dr. Pierce's famous prayer, "Let my heart be broken by the things that break the heart of God."[1] Organizations in difficulty or decline often resort to removing the head person in hopes of improving performance. Whether considering the CEO of a worldwide corporation or the lead pastor of a local congregation, most observers would agree that leadership is very important.

But leadership may matter less than many of us tend to assume. Congregations are complex systems nested in dynamic environments, and no leader—no matter how skilled—is capable of controlling all the variables involved in congregational functioning. Over time congregational dynamics tend to be fairly stable, and the arrival or departure of a given leader generally does not dramatically change a congregation's behavior. As discussed in the introduction, leaders may matter most as *symbols* of the congregation. They set a tone for the congregation and come to symbolize its successes and failures. Leadership is indeed very important, but it is not all-important.

Leaders exist at both the formal and informal level in a congregational system. As discussed in chapter 2, leaders whose positions appear in the organizational chart are presumed to have authority. They are the ones to whom the organization has granted positional power—the right to make certain kinds of decisions according to their job descriptions. Other members may not always respect their authority in the system and other sources of power may trump their positional power. Nonetheless, such positions taken together comprise the formal leadership structure.

Informal leaders also abound in any congregation. The sources of their power may include personal attributes such as intelligence or may derive from access to other powerful individuals or from longevity in the organization. Informal leaders may not possess any formal authority (legitimized power), but their power to influence outcomes in the congregation cannot be denied or overlooked. Given the multiple sources of power in any congregation, it is common to find some individuals who possess both formal positional power and informal personal power.

In addition to the distinction between formal leaders and informal leaders, most congregations also distinguish between ordained leaders and lay leaders. Because not all congregational employees are ordained, the real contrast may be between paid staff and lay volunteers. Regardless of congregational polity, this basic distinction is often a source of tension and at times a source of conflict in congregations. Because paid staff often report to a lay board or committee made up of unpaid volunteers, church staff—and especially lead pastors—may feel like they have a dozen or even a hundred bosses.

Sources of power and leadership positions are thus multiple in congregations—informal and formal, volunteer and paid, lay and clergy. Healthy congregations tend to talk openly about power and seek to distribute it widely. This does not imply a flat organizational chart, meaning that no one position is above any other. Rather, it suggests that highly functioning congregational leaders tend to view power as an infinite resource and encourage broadly distributed decision-making authority. When congregational leaders at all levels know that they are capable of making their own decisions about a wide range of issues, power struggles tend to diminish.

This chapter and the research described throughout this book focus primarily on formal, paid congregational leadership—the ordained clergy and church staff. This is not to suggest that formal, paid leadership is always the most important form of congregational leadership. In family-size congregations, for example, long-term informal leadership may exercise greater power than paid clergy. In such congregations, church consultants quip that "pastors come and go, but the church boss lives on forever." Pastors in family-size congregations often confessed that they were not the key leaders in their systems. As one pastor of a family-size congregation reported, "There's a powerful old guard that runs the congregation."

For most pastoral-size or larger congregations, however, ordained, salaried pastors hold the most visible and vulnerable leadership function in the system.[2] Comments from research respondents indicated that many pastors understand their paradoxical and often vulnerable position in the congregational system. If they clearly articulated their own beliefs on some theological or political issues, for example, they risked alienating many members of their congregations. Pastors were also often aware that their visibility within the congregational system made it more likely that they would be credited or blamed for developments. At times they affirmed lay leaders in the church board for standing with them in the face of opposition from others in the congregation. Three of the pastors I interviewed provided the following quotes:

- "An elder was attacking me, but the session took more authority to protect the pastor."
- "A group left a year ago, as they were angry with the rector (my predecessor). The vestry stood with the rector against some who wanted him out."
- "Some felt the previous pastor was ousted without sufficient input."

Pastors know that they are visible and thus vulnerable. Perhaps that is why so many pastors snatch up books on leadership and attend seminars designed to increase their effectiveness as leaders.

Leadership Effectiveness

What makes for effective congregational leaders? Countless books on leadership have attempted to answer this question, many written as virtual autobiographies by particular leaders who experienced significant career success. But copying another successful leader's unique style seldom produces copycat success. Rather, research on leaders across organizations may point to more universal characteristics than do particular biographies.

In the heavily researched management book *Good to Great*, Jim Collins and his colleagues selected eleven unusually successful U.S. corporations from among an initial pool of more than a thousand companies and attempted to isolate all the factors that led to their remarkable success. Among the organizational factors they identified was a particular leadership style common to all eleven of the leaders who headed the companies during their transition from "good to great." Collins dubbed these leaders "Level 5 leaders," but all were characterized by a striking combination of a very strong will (on behalf of the organization) and a quiet personal humility.

According to Collins and his research team, the Level 5 leaders did not seek their own success or visibility, but were unwavering in their pursuit of what was best for their organizations. They often possessed a crystal clear vision of where the company should be headed, but they combined that vision with humility about their own role in leading the organization. In interviews with these leaders, the researchers were often struck by how these demonstrably successful leaders would change the subject if it became too focused on them. In contrast with the charismatic, larger-than-life leader often brought in from the outside to transform an organization, these highly effective leaders were often homegrown—having spent years working quietly and competently within the organization.[3]

Within organizational psychology and management theory, four other research traditions have emerged to explain the functioning of organizational leaders. These four traditions were summarized by Stephen Zaccaro and Richard Klimoski in their 2001 book, *The Nature of Organizational Leadership: Understanding the Performance Imperatives Confronting Today's Leaders.*[4] The four traditions purported to explain leadership effectiveness are as follows:

- Social and interpersonal exchange
- Strategic management
- Organizational systems
- Leader effectiveness

The first tradition that Zaccaro and Klimoski discuss, *social and interpersonal exchange,* focuses primarily on the relationship between the leader and his or her followers. Effective leaders are seen as those who skillfully manage interpersonal relationships.

Research in this tradition tends to be acontextual—ignoring both other organizational variables and the environment in which the organization is operating.

The focus of *strategic management* is the strategic decision-making activities of top executives and particularly the proactive efforts of managers to align the organization with its dynamic environment. The emphasis in this research tradition is thus on executive planning processes, and the underlying assumption is that leaders' strategic thinking is what most determines organizational outcomes.

The *organizational systems* approach describes organizations as interconnected, organic systems embedded in particular environments. According to Zaccaro and Klimoski, the systems approach "emphasizes the role of the leader in coordinating and maintaining system interconnectiveness and promoting system adaptiveness to external change."[5] From this perspective, top managers who understand and manage their organizations as organic systems embedded in dynamic environments are the most likely to succeed.

The *leader effectiveness* tradition focuses entirely on the internal traits and qualities of leaders that are seen as predictive of executive effectiveness or success. Zaccaro and Klimoski cite research from the Center for Creative Leadership that found that managers "who put personal advancement ahead of personal integrity, had weak interpersonal skills, and were narrowly focused in terms of technical and cognitive skills were more likely to fail after reaching higher levels of management," compared to their colleagues who did not exhibit these traits.[6]

Despite the apparent distinctiveness of these four research traditions, the first and last cohere in their focus on the internal and relational traits of the manager, while the second and third both emphasize managers proactively adapting to a dynamic environment. Leadership effectiveness, then, has been studied on the basis of internal qualities and interpersonal skills as well as environmental awareness and the ability to adapt strategically. As a whole, leadership research suggests that successful leaders skillfully manage themselves and their interactions with others while simultaneously monitoring their organization's dynamic environment and proactively adapting their organization to that environment.[7] The process of adapting an organization to its environment is what is more commonly called leading congregational change.

Leadership and Change

In my organizational consulting experience, organizations tend not to make major changes unless and until their leaders change. Such change may mean replacing an existing leader or may consist of other internal changes within the leader or leadership team. A congregation is likely to make changes to its decision-making structure or worship format only with the approval, and often with the advocacy, of its top leader or its leadership team. Major decisions in congregational life are generally referred to the board on which the pastor or priest sits and over which this leader may preside. If the leader is opposed to or uncomfortable with the proposed change, it is normally denied or at least deferred.

Changes to major areas such as the decision-making structure or to the worship practices of a congregation would thus occur only with leadership sanction, if not full support. Therefore, members of a congregational system will logically conclude that leaders truly are responsible for the changes they are experiencing. The majority in any congregation will take a wait-and-see attitude on major change efforts, withholding judgment until the results are in. If those changes go well, leaders will be praised. If they do not go well—or are simply opposed by a significant portion of the organization's membership—leaders may be

condemned. Leaders thus tend to get the credit when things go
well and condemnation when they don't.

One of the most visible ways in which a congregation con-
demns its leader is by asking for the leader's termination. Some
leaders sense the impending rejection and choose to depart before it becomes official. We would therefore expect that turnover
of the lead pastor and other employed staff would correlate with
changes to decision-making structure and to worship. It does.[8]

Changes to Structure and Worship

In the 36 cases in which respondents reported a change in decision-making structure, only four occurred in congregations
where no staff turnover was reported, while 32 (nearly 90 percent) took place in congregations that also reported staff turnover. In the remaining 64 congregations with no reported changes
in decision-making structure just 43 congregations (67 percent)
experienced staff turnover. Staff turnover was thus significantly
more likely to occur in congregations that also changed their
decision-making structure.

Of the 26 congregations that experienced both a change to
the decision-making structure and a conflict, in 18 cases (nearly
70 percent) the conflict occurred either in the same year as or
sometime following the changes to decision making. In only 8
cases did the conflict precede (and in some cases precipitate) the
change to decision-making structure. The causal relationship is
thus generally (70 percent of the time) as follows:

Changes to Decision Making ➤ Conflict ➤ Pastoral Staff Turnover

What are the mechanisms that may be at work in this phenomenon? Structural changes in congregations are generally
initiated by leading staff members, and people who experience

those changes negatively will tend to blame the person(s) who initiated them. If some congregational members feel that they have lost or are at risk of losing power due to a restructuring process, we should not be surprised if they direct their displeasure about the loss to those whom they view as primarily responsible for it.

Of the 42 cases in which respondents reported adding and/or deleting a worship service in the previous five years, only 2 occurred in congregations that reported no staff changes, and the remainder (95 percent) occurred in congregations that reported staff changes. By comparison, of the 58 congregations that reported no new or dropped worship services, only 35 (60 percent) experienced staff turnover. However, given that the addition of a worship service also correlated with large church size and that larger churches experience greater staff turnover, we cannot claim that changes to worship alone produced the higher level of turnover.[9]

Correlation is not causation, and a significant limitation of this study is that I failed to ask for the date the reported worship change occurred. However, I would offer the following deductive hypothesis:

1. Conflict was more than twice as likely to occur in congregations that added or deleted a worship service during the five-year study period as in congregations that did not.

2. For those congregations that experienced both conflict and the addition of a worship service, staff turnover involving the senior pastor or a music director occurred following the reported conflict in more than half the cases.

3. Therefore, congregational staff persons responsible for music and worship—including the senior pastor—appear to be more vulnerable to reduced tenure if they are also seen as responsible for the initiation or termination of a worship service.

Determining the degree to which these congregational employees deserved their reduction in tenure is impossible. Perhaps the planning or implementation processes for the new worship services were mishandled in some if not many of the cases. Processes might have been poorly planned and sensitivities ignored. Additionally, whether due to insufficient resources or to inadequate worship leadership, the quality of the new worship service might have disappointed some or many members. Regardless, conflict correlates with changes to worship, and leadership turnover correlates with conflict.

Conflict and Staff Turnover

Conflict correlates with changes to structure and worship, as it does with departure of a leader. But what can we say about the causal direction? Which comes first, the conflict or the leader's departure?

Of the 45 congregations that reported at least one conflict during the five-year period covered by the study, 27 of the single or initial cases (60 percent) involved conflicts that preceded or occurred in the same year as a staff transition. Of the 18 remaining cases, 9 involved conflicts that followed staff transitions and the other 9 either did not involve any staff transitions or the chronological sequence could not be determined. In short, it appears from this study that conflict is somewhat more likely to precede or at least to accompany staff transitions than it is to follow them. When conflict flares in a congregation, someone on staff is at risk of leaving. The study did not explore whether those who leave do so voluntarily or involuntarily.

Who is likely to leave? This study found that among the 45 conflicted congregations, 25 reported a transition involving the senior pastor and 15 reported a transition involving a lower-level staff position—most commonly in music and worship, youth

Figure 4.1. Change, conflict, and staff turnover.

.347 (p < .001)	Correlation of adding worship with pastor/staff change
.241 (p < .005)	Correlation of change in decision making with pastor/staff change

Sample size: 100 congregations
Subset: 45 congregations reporting at least one conflict during 2000–2005
p = probability

ministry, or administrative support. In only 5 of the 45 conflicted congregations did staff turnover not occur.[10] In 9 of the 23 congregations that added a worship service and experienced conflict, the senior pastor position transitioned following the reported conflict, and in another 4 cases a music director position turned over following the reported conflict.

Considering the correlation between conflict and changes either to worship or to decision making with the correlation between conflict and staff turnover, I offer the following three hypotheses:

1. When congregations make a change to either their worship or decision-making structure, ordained leaders are generally deeply involved in the change process and are often perceived as the initiators of the change.
2. Whether the change process itself is well planned or poorly planned, there will be some, if not significant, resistance due to the disruption of ritual (adding or deleting a worship service) or redistribution of power (decision-making changes).
3. Once resistance appears in the congregation, it is likely to focus not only on the change process itself but also on the leader (ordained or nonordained) who is seen as most responsible for it.

This research project began as an exploration of the effects of a variety of changes on conflict in congregations. Congregational change may originate in the environment and in a congregational system's desire to adapt to demographic changes and changing preferences. But ultimately the change occurs within the congregation itself. A new and more contemporary worship service emerges. Decision making is distributed to teams rather than the traditional board and committee structure. A congregation's subsequent conflict experience may have more to do with how the change process itself is managed than with any other variable.

One of the survey respondents shared an example from his congregation's experience that illustrates the correlation among change, conflict, and the departure of staff. Some of the details have been altered to disguise the congregation.

> This program-size congregation already had two worship services each Sunday morning—one more traditional and the second more contemporary. Some of the under-thirty members of the congregation, however, asserted that the so-called contemporary service might have been so in the 1960s, but that something much more up-to-date was needed in the twenty-first century.
>
> Led by a younger associate pastor, they began to advocate the initiation of a third "truly contemporary" worship service to be offered Saturday nights. This third service would feature rock and rap music and video clips running simultaneously with the pastor's message. Although the proponents had argued that new community members would come to this third service, the major result seemed to be a decline in attendance at the Sunday morning contemporary service and an accompanying shift to the Saturday evening service.
>
> Within a matter of months, however, the third service fizzled and died due to declining participation. A vocal contingent of the congregation's board called attention to

the young associate pastor's role in pushing the new service, including his unwillingness to "receive counsel" during the process of beginning the service. Within several more months, the associate pastor had resigned due to the pressure on him from these lay leaders. Poorly managed change seemed, in this case, to correlate directly with the departure of the staff person deemed most responsible for the change.

Overall attendance at this congregation also declined following what the respondent described as "the Saturday night massacre." The abrupt addition of a third service—followed by its elimination and the equally abrupt departure of the associate pastor—produced a net loss of attendees.

If congregational leaders are to better manage such changes, they need to study the theory and research on organizational change. Fortunately, both congregational studies and biblical stories offer significant insights into how and why congregations change. And because change tends to precede conflict, then congregations also need to develop a practice of change congruent with their deepest values and beliefs. (If the change process matches the deepest values and beliefs of the congregation, conflict is less likely, because the change effort is viewed by most members as legitimate.) This will be the focus of the next chapter. Before addressing a theology of change and conflict, however, I want to summarize one of the most powerful biblical examples of leadership in a time of change and conflict.

The Jerusalem Council—James's Role

The pressure between the two factions in the early church had been building for years. Paul and his compatriots were evangelizing among Gentiles, teaching them that only faith in the risen Christ was necessary for salvation. Meanwhile, some of those from Judea who continued in their Jewish beliefs and traditions were horrified by the lack of concern Paul showed for instructing these new believers in Jewish law.

The conflict came to a head in Antioch, where the followers of Jesus were first called "Christians." According to the first two verses of Acts 15, "certain individuals" came from Judea to Antioch and instructed the new believers that unless they were circumcised according to the custom taught by Moses, they could not be saved. Paul and Barnabas strongly objected to this teaching, bringing them into a "sharp dispute and debate" with the contingent from Judea. Direct negotiation proved fruitless, so the dispute was sent to the apostles and elders in Jerusalem for resolution.

The sequence of events at the Jerusalem Council is fascinating, albeit sketchy. First, some of the believers from the "party of the Pharisees" presented their allegation against Paul and Barnabas, based on the premise that the "Gentiles must be circumcised and required to keep the law of Moses" (15:5).[11] Second, the apostles and elders who had gathered in Jerusalem convened to consider this highly conflictual issue and then engaged in "much discussion" (15:7). Only after this discussion and apparently after a consensus had been reached did a series of more public speeches commence.

The first to speak was Peter, who himself had experienced a revelation regarding Gentile believers during his vision on the rooftop of Simon's house in Joppa and subsequent visit to Cornelius's house in Caesarea (Acts 10). Peter reminded those gathered in Jerusalem that God had given the Holy Spirit to Gentiles as well as Jews and concluded that it was "through the grace of our Lord Jesus that we are saved, just as they are" (Acts 15:11). Given the ongoing tension between Paul and Peter, this was a striking affirmation of Pauline teaching by his adversary. Paul and Barnabas went next, recounting examples they had seen of God at work among Gentile believers. The stories must have been quite compelling, because "the whole assembly became silent" as they spoke (Acts 15:12).

Only after Peter, Paul, and Barnabas finished speaking did James speak. James was the leader of the church in Jerusalem and very probably had presided over the council's earlier private discussion and consensus building. James first affirmed Peter's comments and connected the conversion of Gentiles with the words of the prophet Amos. He then articulated the negotiated agreement that had likely been reached through the earlier discussion. Gentile believers did not need to be circumcised, James proposed, but would need to respect four dietary and sexual practice laws that were important to Jewish believers. This compromise agreement was written in a letter and sent along with two emissaries to Gentile believers in Antioch, Syria, and Cilicia (Acts 15:23).

It doesn't appear that this careful compromise fully resolved the issue of how Gentile believers would be accepted into what had been a Jewish movement. Paul's later confrontation of Peter (recorded in Galatians 2:11–16) suggests that he felt Peter had seriously backslidden in his earlier commitment to fully accept Gentile believers (due to pressure from "the circumcision group"). But it did open the Christian church to the full inclusion of Gentiles and ultimately to the greater growth of the church in Gentile areas than in Jewish ones.

As a model of an effective leader of change, James's example is truly remarkable. Rather than avoiding the conflict sparked by the party of the Pharisees, James provided them with a forum before a convened council in Jerusalem. Instead of dominating the discussion with his own perspective, James created space for considerable discussion—including public presentations by Peter, Paul, and Barnabas. Finally, instead of allowing a free-for-all debate in front of a larger audience, James brought what was likely a carefully negotiated agreement and presented it with his full endorsement. James serves as an early example of what family systems theory would today dub a "well-defined leader."

Traits of Successful Leaders

In twenty-five years of work both within organizations and as an organizational and congregational consultant, I have noted five traits of successful leaders. All have to do with awareness or skills, and thus all can be developed or improved by current leaders. As recommendations for congregational leaders, these traits could be framed as follows: become self-aware, invite disagreement, self-define, think systems, and know your environment.

Successful leaders become self-aware. Without exception, the most destructive leaders I have encountered in my conflict consulting practice have been remarkably unaware of their impact on others. At the extreme would be leaders who commit sexual misconduct with less powerful members of the organization—convinced that the relationship is mutual and empowering. Healthy leaders, by contrast, are consistently aware of others and of their impact on them, and they monitor their own behavior to ensure healthy interaction.

Successful leaders invite disagreement. Successful leaders demonstrate in a variety of ways that they value input and feedback and create mechanisms to encourage such input. Whether through an open door policy or through skillful listening, healthy leaders demonstrate that they care deeply about the views of other congregational members. Leaders who communicate a "you're either for me or against me" mentality inevitably find that they cut out critical feedback—the kind most needed to avoid disastrous decisions.

Successful leaders self-define. Successful congregational leaders are not only good listeners; they also are clear with others in the congregation about their own preferences, values, and dreams. The dean of congregational consultants, Speed Leas of the Alban Institute, found through his numerous cases that pastors became the focus of conflict for two reasons—either they were authoritarian and people felt dominated and ignored, or they refused to self-define and people became frustrated and angry, not knowing what the leaders really believed. Healthy leaders communicate their own preferences; they also invite other congregational members to share theirs.

Successful leaders think systems. Successful congregational leaders tend to think of their congregations as integrated systems and not as isolated parts. Even a leader who heads a particular department or program is likely to be more effective if he can visualize and verbalize his own piece of the congregational puzzle in relationship with other pieces. Granted, this systems view becomes easier to adopt the higher one goes in a congregation. But top congregational leaders can encourage others in the system to grow in their ability to be systems thinkers through workshops, systemwide meetings, and mentoring programs that cross programmatic boundaries.

Successful leaders know their environment. In addition to a deep awareness of themselves and their systems, successful congregational leaders also carefully monitor the changing environments in which their congregation operates. The successful pastor monitors both the changing needs of her members as well as the dynamic environment in which the congregation operates.

Leadership may be more art than science, but successful congregational leaders tend to be aware of and closely monitor their own behavior and that of their congregations. They communicate clearly with congregational members and invite disagreement from any who might see things differently. Finally, they constantly scan the various environments in which their congregations exist and make proactive changes consistent with the congregation's mission, vision, and values.[12]

Even effective leaders may not escape being framed as the "identified patient" if the changes they propose are not successful. But as James's conduct at the Jerusalem council illustrates, leaders who invite disagreement and then build a consensus while clearly articulating their own vision are more likely to help their congregations undergo positive transformation than are leaders who have not learned these skills. In the following chapter we will explore how to create positive change in ways congruent with Christian theology and less likely to produce destructive conflict.

CHAPTER 5

Change and Conflict

This book addresses the relationship between change and conflict. Conflict is visible. Conflict attracts attention. When conflict surfaces in a congregation, congregational leaders notice. But conflict is useful primarily as a visible symptom of underlying congregational dynamics. As noted in the previous three chapters, when change occurs in the decision-making structure of the congregation or in the weekly worship service, conflict is likely to result. Congregational leaders—particularly ordained clergy—are then at risk of becoming the focus of the conflict. Whether deserved or not, ordained leaders tend to be blamed for perceived failures in most congregations. Most congregational crashes, as Friedman observed, tend to be blamed on "pilot error."

As the research cited in this book demonstrates, the primary causes of congregational conflict relate to change. Such changes may appear first in the environment as a congregational system is affected by demographic changes and individuals' changing preferences. But ultimately the change occurs in the context of the congregation itself. A new and more contemporary worship service emerges. Decision making is distributed to teams rather than the traditional board and committee structure. How the change process itself is managed may have more to do with the subsequent conflict experience of the congregation than any other variable.

So how can leaders initiate and manage change processes in ways that reduce destructive conflict and increase the likelihood that desired changes will stick? Fortunately, both organizational sociology and congregational studies offer significant insights into how and why organizations like congregations change. But social science insights are not sufficient motivations for congregations established on Christian beliefs and practices. Congregations also need to develop a theology of change congruent with their deepest values and beliefs. I will address theories of change from the social sciences first, followed by a theology of change that draws on Christian Scripture, tradition, and sacraments.

How and Why Do Congregations Change?

How do we know when congregational change has taken place? Remembering the words of organizational sociologists Paul DiMaggio and Walter Powell, we observe that when a change occurs in the structure, culture, or strategy of a congregation, then congregational change has indeed transpired.[1] In other words, when a congregation restructures, attempts to change its culture (particularly through the introduction of a new worship service), or engages in a meaningful strategic planning process—change has occurred.

Why do congregations change? In the memorable words of congregational researcher Nancy Ammerman, organizational change is a result of survival of the *fittest*, survival of the *similar*, or survival of the *savvy*.[2] If change is a result of survival of the fittest, those congregations that best adapt to the changing needs of their geographic environment and exploit their general or specific niche will experience the most success. If change is a result of survival of the similar, those congregations that best align with their institutional environments will thrive. And if change is a result of survival of the savvy, those congregations whose

leaders best manage the external dependencies of the congregation (for resources like members and money) will prevail.

As a group, congregations that experienced growth during
the five-year period considered by the study gave evidence of all
three mechanisms of change. Some adapted their worship services to appeal to a younger constituency in their geographic
environment. Others adopted team-based models of decision
making that illustrated institutional theory's assertion that organizations attempt to align their structures with their institutional environment. Finally, some congregational leaders seemed
particularly adept at attracting new members and resources in
ways that transcended changes to either structure or worship.
Given that one theory can't accommodate all the reasons congregational change might occur, a multifaceted frame such as
Ammerman's is particularly helpful in understanding why congregations change. But how can congregational leaders ensure
that their efforts at change are effective and lasting?

Effective Change Management

"Change is not made without inconvenience, even from worse to
better," said the eighteenth-century English writer Samuel Johnson. After all, organizations like congregations develop habits (patterns of thinking and behaving) because they are efficient. It takes
less time and energy to respond in a familiar way than an unfamiliar one. Change efforts should therefore not be undertaken on
a whim. As many survivors of organizational downsizing efforts
could attest, major change is too costly, too anxiety producing, and
too destabilizing to undergo unless it is truly necessary.

There are, however, some times when a congregation needs
to commit to a change process. Congregational leaders are well
advised to initiate a proactive change process when they witness
the following developments:

- When the external *environment*, which includes the surrounding geographic environment as well as the larger societal environment, changes.
- When the basic purpose or *mission* of the congregation changes, such as from primarily serving the needs of commuting members to primarily reaching out to a surrounding neighborhood.
- When the way congregational employees do their work (*process*) needs to change—often precipitated by changes in the technological environment.
- When the *structure or culture* of the congregation has become an obstacle to the congregation's accomplishing its mission.

In short, times occur when congregational leaders need to take the initiative in leading their congregations through a managed change process. Such a process may be part of a regular strategic planning effort—often undertaken every three to five years, or it may take place separate from a formal planning process. Regardless, the basic components of a successful change process are fairly well established in the organizational management literature. A number of "stage models" of planned organizational change exist, but most are predicated upon the following three assumptions.

First, organizations won't make major changes unless they perceive an urgent, often life-threatening, need to do so. Even then, the change will be resisted by some in the organization. Second, organizational change is not accomplished by one person, even when she or he is the top leader. A broad-based coalition is needed to bring about change. Finally, successful change efforts are characterized by communication and participation. Organizational members will need opportunities not only to hear about the proposed changes but also to help shape them.

If You Build, Will They Fight?

One of the most striking findings from this research was the lack of any significant statistical correlation between building projects and conflict. Both theoreticians and practitioners have argued that major building projects produce conflict. From a theoretical perspective, the significant change in physical structure that accompanies most building projects should be enough to engender conflict. And consultants who work with congregations often warn ominously about the conflict that should be expected in the wake of a building project—often presumed to include the departure of the senior pastor. Yet in this study, the 46 congregations that undertook major building projects did not experience conflict at a significantly higher rate than the 54 that did not.[3] Why not?

I believe three variables account for this lack of increased conflict. These three variables illustrate two of the three points from the change management literature (building a supporting coalition and immersing change efforts in communication and participation). The third variable owes more to the earlier discussion about the importance of ritual in Christian congregations.

First, congregational leaders have been warned for decades about the risk of conflict presumed to accompany building projects. Therefore, they tend to carefully plan the process, slowly build a supporting coalition, often rely on outside consultants, and anticipate and prepare for disagreement and conflict.

Second, congregational leaders recognize that major transitions occur when a new building is constructed or an older one substantially renovated. Leaders thus tend to communicate with those who will be affected by the transition and negotiate how the new space will be utilized. As the building itself rises or is remade, members have time to adjust to the pending changes.

Finally, most congregations ritualize the transition from an old building to a new one. Groundbreaking ceremonies are inevitably scheduled when work finally begins on the new worship center. On the day the transition is formalized, a farewell service is often held in the old facility, and members are often invited to walk from the old building to the new one, symbolizing the loss of one significant place and the acquisition of another.

I believe what congregations and their leaders have learned about how to handle the transitions involved in major building projects must now be applied to other major congregational transitions—such as changes to worship or decision making. Not only must a significant transition process be carefully planned with participation by key stakeholders, but a congregation must also find ways to ritualize the inevitable endings and new beginnings that accompany major change. Simply announcing the transition to team ministry after decades of bureaucratic committees will not be enough. The significant contribution of those committee leaders—and of the committee structure itself—must be recognized and ritualized. Those congregations who ignore their previous patterns in the rush to adopt new ones are condemned to experience conflict. Old patterns don't simply fade away. Rather, they resist tenaciously unless recognized graciously.

The learnings from building projects regarding the importance of process and ritual also apply to pastoral and other staff transitions. By and large, most congregations have learned to ritualize the arrivals and departures of staff. But the significant correlation between staff departures and congregational conflict in this study remains troubling. Certainly pastors and other staff may depart due to poorly managed conflict in the congregation. But some of the correlation may be due to inadequate attention to process—particularly poorly managed beginnings. Consistent with Roy Pneuman's warning about the "new pastor who rushes into changes," pastors beginning a new charge would be well advised to study the congregation and build relationships before initiating major changes.[4] Leaders have to earn the right to make changes. Once they have earned the right to begin a major change process, effective leaders will build a supporting coalition and organize a careful and open process to plan and implement the change.

Earning the Right to Make Changes

A young pastor was called to serve a medium-sized congregation of about 200 members located in a suburban community. She had previously served as an associate pastor under an experienced senior pastor and learned the importance of both going slowly when making cultural changes and modeling the desired changes. In her new assignment, she encountered an entrenched congregational culture that valued harmony and agreement but had no tolerance for disagreement or dissent. When disagreement did surface, it was expressed through intense bursts of anger that left everyone wary of conflict.

The pastor committed first to learning the culture and understanding the rules and roles in the congregation. Because she had studied anthropology in college, the role of "participant observer" came naturally to her. She asked questions, tested observations, and in general demonstrated her interest in learning more about the congregation and its ways of being.

Within several years the pastor had earned the respect of the congregation and with that respect the right to make changes. She decided to concentrate first on the board that met monthly with her as well as with two other staff in the congregation. The pastor worked with the staff and the board to develop a "relational covenant" that described how they wanted to work together and how they would deal with disagreements and conflict when they arose. More important, the pastor modeled the behavior called for in the covenant—inviting others to respectfully disagree with her and demonstrating what such disagreement would look like.

The change in the congregational culture was slow but noticeable. After a challenging meeting in which a major proposal for structural change was debated and all members present spoke during a circle process, one long-term member remarked on the changes she had observed. "We never would have a discussion like this five years ago," she said. "Either the people who were opposed would have sat there in angry silence, or they would have erupted with accusations, and the leaders would have gotten defensive. This time, you welcomed their concerns, and they were expressed appropriately."

Because of her willingness to learn the system, to earn the right to make change, and to work with leadership as a group, this pastor successfully changed the culture of a congregation with dysfunctional conflict habits. Even after she left, the new habits continued as the expression of a changed conflict culture.

Managing the Transition Zone

A more recent development in the literature on organizational change is the awareness that during any significant change process, things usually get worse before they get better. According to management authors David M. Schneider and Charles Goldwasser, "During any transition, performance will inevitably decline before reaching the improved desired state. . . . Managing change is really about managing this transition."[5] A remarkable number of organizational change efforts are aborted in the middle of this "transition zone," mainly because organizational leaders succumb to resistance efforts and the demonstrably lowered morale and performance in the midst of major transitions. So how can leaders successfully implement changes—even major ones—that are indeed necessary for the health and future of the congregation?

Success stories of a highly principled leader single-handedly transforming an entire system exist primarily in fictional literature and the movies. The reality is that planned change generally happens when leaders (informal or formal) form coalitions that cross traditional organizational lines. Whether dubbed a "guiding coalition," a "strategic planning task force," or a "change management committee," a group of five to ten dedicated volunteers recruited from across the organization to study the situation and make recommendations is more likely than any single leader to achieve lasting change.

Such groups have their drawbacks, as anyone who has served time on a strategic planning or structure review committee can attest. But if top leaders actively participate in or at least bless the group process, if skilled process leadership is present, and if a timeline is developed and followed, the likelihood of success is appreciably increased. Successful change happens when a broad-based coalition—viewed as legitimate across the system—takes on a major challenge with a limited timeframe and develops realistic recommendations. Yet we all know of committee or consultant reports that contain brilliant recommendations but are only gathering dust on a manager's shelf. Despite the enormous effort invested in the information-gathering and analysis stage, as well as the careful thought that went into the recommendations, nothing changes. Why?

Brilliant recommendations developed by broad-based coalitions alone are not sufficient. In addition, leaders need to develop an implementation strategy and model the desired behaviors, including managing their own anxiety around the proposed change. Congregations ultimately change when leaders change. Change may occur when one leader leaves and another comes, such as when one lead pastor is replaced by another. But it can just as easily occur when congregational leaders change their behaviors despite continuing in their roles. The key is that congregational leaders need to model the behaviors desired in the broader system. As leaders change their behaviors, the culture of the congregation will begin to shift.

This takes us to Mahatma Gandhi's simple dictum, "Be the change you wish to see."[6] One might argue with this truism if she is thinking only of the case of a single citizen in a large country, but the saying certainly applies to congregational leaders. Put simply, leaders need to model in their own behaviors and interactions the desired changes they wish to see. If leaders want a culture where every congregational member takes responsibility for his or her own behavior, they need to begin modeling what such responsibility-taking behavior might look like. And if they desire a decision-making structure that pushes decision making to the lowest possible level, they need to both change structures and delegate authority. Congregations change when leaders change.

Fear and Change

Yet a deeper level of insight key to understanding change and resistance is needed. Congregational practitioner and scholar Jeff Woods begins his essay "New Tasks for the New Congregation: Reflections on Congregational Studies" with this assertion: "Today's congregations now function in a postmodern, multigenerational, multicultural world."[7] Having named the environment (and later defined the terms), Woods proceeds to detail the implications of a changed environment for congregations in this postmodern society. These include:

- Shift towards images rather than facts
- Emphasis on experience rather than reason
- Acceptance of competing sources of truth

Woods's understanding of adaptation to environmental change is colorful. "Within every shifting landscape," he writes, "are those units that survive by their innovation and those other units that die by their stubbornness."[8] He notes that congregations in the United States today contain proportionally more women, more retired individuals, and more married couples than the general population and concludes that congregations are reaching a subset of the population but failing to adapt to significant changes in the population. Woods then details five tasks for "the twenty-first-century congregation," each of which implies significant change to the ways most congregations now function.

Woods is particularly sober regarding the consequences of fundamental change in congregations. He equates change management with pain management, concluding that a congregation's ability to embrace major change will depend upon its threshold for pain. Woods quotes Nancy Ammerman: "You can't change without undergoing conflict. The congregations that systematically avoid conflict are not going to be able to change."[9] Congregations that fear conflict and are unable to face the pain of changing will thus likely refuse to change and will not adapt to a rapidly changing environment.

Here I believe is the second link between change and conflict. The first link, discussed at length in earlier chapters, is between changes to the decision-making structure and worship and the resulting conflict. But this second link is more primordial. It is between the prospect of change in a congregation and the *fear* that destructive conflict will result. The fear of conflict then acts as glue, preventing significant change initiatives from emerging and stifling normal adaptation processes.

Congregational leaders, then, may face two unattractive options as they consider the need for change in their congregational systems: (1) initiate the change, knowing that some or many members may resist the initiative and that conflict is likely to result; and (2) defer the change out of a desire to avoid the feared conflict but knowing that failing to adapt to a changing environment may lead to decline and eventually even congregational death.

Given these two options, how can leaders equip themselves and other congregational members to deal with the nearly constant changes that are affecting our society and our congregations? In an era of outsourcing and rightsizing, congregational members can be forgiven for looking at change a bit skeptically, if not fearfully. When the rate of change is high and the environment is complex, congregational members will experience very high levels of uncertainty and anxiety. Managing uncertainty and anxiety is thus the essential task for leaders who want to either initiate or manage change.

Because leaders do indeed set the tone in congregations, leaders' ability to manage their own anxiety will determine—more than any other single factor—the group's ability to manage its anxiety. Congregational members may not always listen to what leaders *say*, but they are constantly watching what they *do*. If leaders are able to honestly name the uncertainty inherent in managing change while demonstrating openness and flexibility to the changes that are occurring, they will send a signal that pending changes need not be feared or avoided.

This discussion can be summarized in four principles of change in organizations: (1) like people, congregations will generally only change when the pain of not changing exceeds the pain and inconvenience of changing; (2) managing change starts with managing oneself, including one's own anxiety; (3) building a coalition is necessary for successful and sustainable change; and (4) congregations change when leaders change.

"Change or die" is too simple a slogan, but it communicates something of the dilemma that congregational leaders face. Considering this stark alternative, congregations, I believe, need to look beyond either organizational theories or congregational studies to find their way forward. They need to look to their own deepest beliefs, values, and traditions.

A Theology of Change

Christian congregations tend to trace their core values to the founder of their religion, Jesus of Nazareth, and to the Christian Scriptures that contain his teaching. And they are much more likely to refer to interpretations of the founder's teaching and behavior as a "theology" rather than a "theory." A shared theology can motivate action in a congregation, whereas a theory generates mostly indifference. So what might a theology of change look like for Christian congregations?

Richard McCorry, a Roman Catholic lay minister and author, responds to this question in *Dancing with Change: A Spiritual Response to Changes in the Church.*[10] McCorry identifies three sources of support for congregations undertaking a significant change effort—tradition, ritual, and Scripture. Because each is embraced by the culture of most Christian congregations, I believe they resonate with the call from many organizational change experts to "embed the change in the culture."

Despite the reputation of many religious traditions as conservative bastions endeavoring to maintain the status quo, McCorry argues that in fact the major religious traditions (including Christianity) are mostly about change. Jesus called his first disciples to drop what they were doing and follow him. Those who profess to follow Christ have throughout the past two millennia been instructed to repent (turn around) and become new creatures. The church itself, and particularly the Roman Catholic Church as an institution, may indeed be a conservative force in the world. The teachings of the tradition, however, are immersed in change.

The rituals or sacraments of the church also often serve to mark significant events of individual and community change. Mc-Corry observes that the sacraments are rituals for times of transition and that "in many ways we sacramentalize our change."[11] In addition to the obvious rituals such as infant dedications, weddings, and funerals that accompany major life transitions, the routine rituals of the church (baptism and the Eucharist) are also change markers. For McCorry, "Baptism captures one of the central paradoxes of the Christian faith. When those baptized go into the water, they are said to have died to sin. When they come out of the water, they are said to have risen with Christ."[12]

Likewise, the celebration of the Eucharist (or communion) in most Christian traditions is a regular reminder of the essential transformation at the heart of the Christian belief system. "Christ has died, Christ has risen, Christ will come again" is a synopsis of the three stages of the change process stressed in models developed by several organizational change experts. For one of those experts, William Bridges, success in managing change comes with the ability to recognize that something old is dying and that something new is taking its place. In the middle, however, is a "neutral zone" where performance and morale inevitably deteriorate as organizational members let go of something familiar and adapt to something unfamiliar.[13]

McCorry applies the pascal mystery (Easter story) to this three-stage model. Jesus's death on what Christians commemorate as Good Friday represents the dying stage of the change process. His followers' confusion and fear on Holy Saturday captures the inevitable resistance and anxiety that accompanies the neutral zone. Finally, the resurrection that Christians celebrate on Easter Sunday parallels the new beginning that characterizes successful organizational change. However, without the letting go on Friday and the confusion and grief on Saturday, the new life on Sunday would not be meaningful. The heart of Christian theology thus equips church members to enter the hard work of transitioning required in a genuine change process.

Finally, Christian Scriptures contain numerous examples of change and conflict, both in response to Jesus's ministry and in the recorded stories of the early church. McCorry points to the account recorded in Acts 15 of conflict over the inclusion of Gentiles in the life of the new movement, which was discussed in the previous chapter. Foreshadowing later arguments over the inclusion of women and gays and lesbians in the life and leadership of the church, the compromise reached in Acts 15 achieved a structural change but not a complete cultural one. Gentiles would now be officially welcomed into the church without having to obey the Mosaic Law, but given Paul's continuing battles with the "Judaizers" there would be ongoing resistance to their full participation.

Scripture, tradition, and rituals thus offer a variety of avenues for congregational leaders who undertake a major change effort. Clergy can explore the stories in Scripture of change, resistance, and conflict from the pulpit and in their teaching ministry. The importance of "forgetting what is behind and straining toward what is ahead" can be intoned from the core traditions of the faith itself (Phil. 3:13). Perhaps most important, congregational leaders can access the rich reservoir of ritual to assist their congregations in making the transition from the known to the unknown.

Conflict in Congregations

We have looked at change in congregations and now will consider the phenomenon that often accompanies change—conflict. Every congregation experiences conflict, even though each one does so in unique ways. The sources of conflict may vary from the micro to the macro—from intrapersonal pathologies to personality differences to globalization forces—but over time they are inescapable. Various studies have shown that organizational leaders and managers spend up to 25 percent of their time managing conflict. Experienced pastors know that during times of crisis, conflict management duties can become all-consuming.

Although many members assume that all congregational conflicts emerge from personality differences or communication problems, other significant sources are often at work within the system itself. These include the factors discussed in the previous three chapters—the structure, culture, and leadership of the organization. However, conflict can result not just from *changes* in the structure, culture, and environment but also from other systemic realities *within* those three areas.

Conflict can arise out of the congregational *structure* from one of several causes. First, conflict results when power is overly centralized and those with less power attempt to shift the power imbalance. Second, roles can be so poorly defined that overlapping and thus contested responsibilities lead to tension and conflict. Third, the formal and the informal social structure can be so divergent that conflict emerges from differing perceptions of who really has authority. Leaders who notice patterns in the interpersonal conflicts in their congregation will want to consider these possible structural causes.

An organization's *culture* can be another underlying source of conflict, particularly its most visible expression—the worship service. The most common conflict arises when newer congregational members encounter an entrenched organizational culture that they do not share. The conflicts that result tend to be framed by both groups in terms of right and wrong behavior, as culture supplies the values and norms that help us determine what behavior is appropriate or inappropriate. If a pastor or other staff person hired from outside the congregation is perceived to be acting in ways that are counter to the congregation's cultural values, conflict is particularly likely and tends to be acute. (And when an outside leader and an inside culture clash, culture normally wins.)

Finally, the multiple *environments* in which a congregation is nested also provide the potential for multiple sources of conflict. This is the reason why "town/gown" conflicts (between communities and the colleges or universities they host) are so common; academic cultures that value debate and progressive thinking are likely to be in tension with environments that value harmony and traditional values. Universities owned by religious denominations may be particularly prone to internal disputes due to conflicting environments; the religious and cultural environment represented by the founding denomination clashes with the institutional environment represented by the broader academic field—including the secular universities where most professors receive their degrees.

Congregational conflict consultant Speed Leas's Levels of Conflict grid demonstrates how conflict can escalate to destructive levels in an organization like a congregation.[14] The five conflict levels are as follows:

- Level 1—Problem to Solve: Normal issue-focused differences resolved through dialogue
- Level 2—Disagreement: A difference that has not been resolved and is becoming a sharper disagreement that may need to be negotiated
- Level 3—Contest: An unresolved disagreement that has become personalized into what starts being referred to as a "conflict" and may need mediation
- Level 4—Fight or Flight: A conflict that has begun to polarize a group as factions emerge supporting the original two parties. The use of authority or of an outside consultant is normally indicated at this level.
- Level 5—Intractable Situation: A polarized conflict that has spiraled out of control and become highly destruc-

tive. Leas suggests that "separating the parties" may be the indicated strategy at this level of conflict.

Congregational leaders are well advised to attend to conflict at the lower levels and to offer mediation to members of the congregation if a conflict has escalated beyond the first two levels. The danger to the organization from Level 4 or 5 conflicts is so acute that earlier intervention to prevent conflict escalation is the most desirable strategy. Where that is not successful, congregational leaders may need assistance from outside the organization to deescalate the conflict to a more manageable level.

Although conflict is inevitable, many scholars and practitioners believe that any organization may have an optimal level of conflict. Some disagreement and conflict provides energy and generates ideas, but too much conflict becomes destructive. When an organization has too little conflict, it may need to be encouraged, and when an organization has too much conflict, it may need to be reduced. In the middle of this curve, however, lies an optimal level of conflict where most organizations seem to thrive. Stirring the conflict pot may be needed in some situations, but when the pot starts to boil over, a conflict reduction strategy may be needed.

Diagnosing the level of conflict and seeking outside assistance at higher levels constitutes the "intervention" end of the conflict management spectrum. At the "prevention" end lie opportunities for congregational leaders to create a conflict-healthy system where disagreement is welcomed and destructive conflict doesn't take root. A conflict-healthy system includes both individual behaviors and congregational mechanisms to manage conflict. It begins with the recognition that leaders set the tone regarding conflict management in their congregations, along with many other behavioral norms.

An organization's culture matters more than its structure. Therefore, while congregational leaders may be able to create a mediation program or an open-door policy, the greater challenge will likely be changing the conflict culture sufficiently so that congregational members will naturally seek out and use interest-based methods of conflict resolution rather than only choosing flight or fight.[15]

Culture changes when behaviors and assumptions change, and leaders' behaviors and assumptions matter most of all. Therefore, leaders who learn to know the system, build a supporting coalition, and model the desired changes are affecting the culture of their congregations. The culture may at first resist, but leaders' persistence in modeling the desired assumptions and behaviors will over time change the conflict culture—the norms and behaviors around conflict in your congregation. Managing conflict starts with managing oneself. Consider the conflict culture that you would like to have in your congregation, then start behaving as if that culture has already arrived. Culture change is never easy, and it is often painful. But it is possible.[16]

Conflict and Change in Acts 6

A compelling example of leaders' turning conflict into opportunity for structural and cultural change is found in the first seven verses of Acts 6. The idyllic description of the first Christian community, recorded in Acts 2:42–47 and Acts 4:32–37 is soon marred by incidents of deception in Acts 5:1–11 and internal conflict in Acts 6:1–7. While the sudden deaths of Ananias and Sapphira—who attempted to deceive the apostles about the extent of their generosity—are shocking, the conflict recorded in Acts 6 sounds more familiar to our ears. One group murmured (or complained) against another group, and leaders intervened to resolve the conflict.

The complaints came from the Hellenistic or Greek-speaking Jews and were directed against the Aramaic-speaking Jews. Most scholars agree that the Aramaic-speaking Jews were in the majority of the early Christian movement and included the original twelve disciples—now called apostles. The identified issue for the minority group was that their "widows were being overlooked in the daily distribution of food" (Acts 6:1)—a compelling allegation in a society where care for widows and orphans was part of the Mosaic Law.

The twelve apostles could have ignored these allegations, ordered the minority group to stop griping, or issued a decree that all widows would henceforth be fed equal portions. Instead, they convened a meeting of all the disciples and self-defined by clarifying their primary role in the community. "It would not be right for us to neglect the ministry of the word of God in order to wait on tables" (Acts 6:2). They then gave the problem back to the group that originally complained, suggesting that they choose seven individuals "full of the Spirit and wisdom" to care for the feeding of widows (v. 3). Fortunately, the proposal "pleased the whole group" (v. 5), and they chose seven men, all of whom had Greek names—and thus were likely from the group that originally brought the complaint.

It is instructive to note that this passage begins and ends with church growth. The first verse of chapter 6 records that "in those days . . . the number of disciples was increasing," while the last verse of this section concludes that "the word of God spread" and "a large number of [Jewish] priests became obedient to the faith" (v. 7). This is thus a story about a conflict, nested in a story about growth and change. This fascinating, if brief, account of the first recorded church conflict offers at least three significant learnings.

First, *leaders need to move towards conflict, not away from it.* This is consistent with the "inviting disagreement" counsel in chapter 4. Leaders who learn to move towards conflict discover that they have opportunities to resolve issues when those issues are small, rather than attempting to fight fires when they are nearly out of control.

Second, *the identified issue is almost never the real issue.* The allegation from the Greek-speaking minority that their "widows were being overlooked" in the daily food distribution was indeed a compelling one, but it likely was a proxy for a deeper feeling of powerlessness and alienation among the Hellenist members of the early church. All the significant leadership positions (apostles) were held by the Aramaic-speaking majority, and the minority did not know how to exercise their voice other than through "murmuring."

Third, *involve the "complainers" in solving their identified problems.* Note that the apostles did not agree to take care of the problem that had been identified. Rather, they recruited members of the murmuring minority to address the problem. This outcome, as noted in chapter 2 on structure, actually created a new role in the church—that of deacon.

Conflict is often a crisis, but it is also an opportunity. Much depends on our attitude towards conflict. If we expect it to be destructive and awful, it probably will be. But if we anticipate that the conflict may instead be an opportunity for genuine change, we may experience transformation. As Ron Kraybill, the founding director of Mennonite Conciliation Service, has said, conflict may be "an arena of revelation," a time when we hear God's voice as we never have before.

Change, Growth, and Conflict

Returning to the research, we may ask about the relationship among change, growth, and conflict. Congregations that made major changes, even through a major building project, were not guaranteed growth. However, congregations that added a worship service, made changes to their fellowship patterns, or initiated new community projects were more likely to grow than congregations that did not do those things.[17] As we have seen, adding or changing a worship service also correlated with conflict, but changing fellowship patterns had much less of a relationship with conflict, and initiating a new community project was negatively correlated (meaning that it made conflict less likely).

In short, not every change causes conflict. Some, like changing fellowship patterns, seem to have no effect when controlling for other variables. Others, such as initiating community projects, slightly reduce the likelihood of conflict. When a congregation adds or deletes a worship service or changes its decision-making structure, conflict is more likely. But when it looks outward to its community and initiates a program, growth is more likely and conflict less so.

"Where there is change, there is conflict" may be too simple a description. "Where there are insufficiently planned changes to the core meaning-making function and power relationships of the congregation, there is likely to be conflict" may be a less memorable phrase. It seems, however, to be a more accurate conclusion.

CHAPTER 6

Where Do We Go from Here?

Congregations matter in North American social life as well as in the kingdom of God. They gather more people more frequently than any other category of voluntary organizations, and together with other religious institutions collectively administer more financial resources than the remainder of the nonprofit sector put together. Congregations also often experience change and conflict. Serious conflicts tend to result in departures from the congregation—especially of lay members but also of salaried staff. These conflicts can be costly in other ways as well—including the loss of significant financial resources, the disruption of personal relationships, and even schism and decline within a particular congregation.[1]

The research reported in this book found that not all changes that occur within local congregations correlate with conflict. Most congregational changes do not, while some changes correlate more with growth than with conflict. Congregations that expanded ministry in their local communities or that made changes to their fellowship patterns were more likely to experience growth and less likely to experience conflict than congregations that did not make these changes. And some changes that have long been predicted to precipitate conflict—such as building projects—did not show a significant correlation with conflict. Congregations may be resistant to change due in part to a fear of conflict, but this study challenges a presumed correlation between *all* change and conflict.

Even the feared size transition did not correlate significantly with conflict. Congregations that were growing—and even those that transitioned from one size category to another during the previous five years—experienced conflict at about the same rate (45 percent) as congregations that were not growing or did not experience a size transition. The size transitions literature is likely correct that the boundaries between size categories tend to act as barriers to growth, but this study provides no support for the hypothesis that congregations that transcend a size barrier (moving either up or down) are significantly more likely to experience conflict.[2]

When other key organizational variables—such as a congregation's size and age—are considered (controlled for), only changes to the decision-making structure and adding or deleting a worship service significantly correlate with conflict. I explored the possible mechanisms that might explain this correlation in chapters 2 and 3, but let me summarize the basic hypotheses.

Changing the Structure

As discussed in chapter 2, the research found that changes to the decision-making structure of a congregation correlate significantly with conflict. In the literature, structure has been understood both as a rational mechanism for distributing power and making decisions and as a ceremonial device for communicating meaning and legitimacy. I suggest that conflict can arise from changes affecting either of these functions. When changes are made to the decision-making structure of a congregation, the flow of power is likely to be disrupted. As sociologists of religion John Sutton and Mark Chaves discovered, when one group attempts to consolidate power in an organizational system, conflict predictably results as other groups resist that initiative.[3]

Power matters. But in religious congregations, power operates as a nearly invisible currency. Congregational leaders are termed "servants" in many Christian traditions, and the model of Christ as a "servant leader" is heralded. While the intent of this language is to encourage service to others rather than the raw exercise of power, the practical result can be pervasive denial of the existence and distribution of power within the congregational system. When struggles over power arise, conflict resolution can be delayed as all involved deny that the conflict has anything to do with power.

But power struggles are not the only mechanism for explaining the correlation between structural changes and conflict. If structure also functions as "myth and ceremony," then even cosmetic changes to a congregation's familiar structure can disrupt homeostasis and lead to conflict.[4] Boards and committees are a product of the organizational age of U.S. society in the mid-twentieth century, just as teams are a product of the network age in the late twentieth century. Regardless of the institutional model, however, organizational members may become attached not only to their roles in the system but also to the structural model itself.

Thus leaders who undertake changes to congregational structure but fail to understand the power-mediating and ceremonial role of that structure may be at particular risk of precipitating conflict. When we fiddle with structure, we fiddle with power. And when we change structure, we threaten what for some members has become well-established myth and ceremony. As with changes to the worship service, changes to structure should never be undertaken lightly. Ritual may possess transformative properties, but it always resists its own transformation.

Three principles for making effective change processes to a decision-making structure are suggested by this discussion: acknowledge power, anticipate conflict, and provide leadership.

Acknowledge Power

Leaders who wish to successfully change decision-making structures and patterns in their organizations would do well to attend to power dynamics within the organization and to the ways in which the proposed changes may affect current power relationships. Given the importance of naming issues before attempting to negotiate them, leaders who undertake successful change efforts will acknowledge their own power as well as that of others within the system.

Anticipate Conflict

Controlling for other variables, congregations that made changes to their decision-making structures were more than three times as likely to experience conflict than congregations that made no changes to their structures. Therefore, congregational leaders should anticipate that disagreements and conflict will likely result from proposed structural changes and invite disagreement to be directly expressed. When leaders attempt to suppress conflict, they simply drive it underground—where it becomes more destructive.

Provide Leadership

Not surprisingly, when you shake the organizational infrastructure, anxiety flows quickly into the cracks. What anxious systems most need are nonanxious leaders. Family systems theory suggests that leaders who are able to manage their own anxiety and to offer mechanisms for dealing with underlying conflict will experience more successful outcomes. My own consulting experience confirms this.

Changing Worship

As discussed in chapter 3, significant changes to worship—defined as adding or deleting a worship service—also significantly correlated with conflict. I have identified the reasons it was more difficult to establish a causal relationship between changes to worship and conflict than between changes to structure and conflict. But the research still found that nearly 60 percent of the congregations that added a worship service experienced a conflict, compared to less than 40 percent of congregations that did not add a service but did experience conflict.

The hypothesis that smaller congregations that begin a second worship service are at greater risk of conflict than larger congregations was not supported by this study. Congregations that initiated a new worship service experienced conflict at essentially the same rate regardless of their size. The disruption-of-ritual hypothesis offered by Mark Chaves offers a more plausible explanation. As Chaves concluded, "When it comes to assembling a new kind of worship event, it may be easier to start over in a new congregation than fight to change practice in an existing one."[5]

It may indeed be easier to start a new practice than to transform an existing one. But if a congregation fails to adapt to a changing environment, it is risking at least its own growth—and perhaps its ultimate survival. While only 39 percent of the congregations that didn't add a worship service experienced growth, 53 percent of the congregations that did add a service also grew. Adding a worship service correlates with conflict, but it also correlates with growth.[6]

The reader will remember that pastor and writer Shane Hipps suggested that differing worldviews might be another factor propelling the current worship wars. Hipps contends that linear, left-brain, and individualistic approaches to worship characterize traditional services, while circular, right brain, and "tribalistic" approaches are embraced in contemporary services.

If Hipps's worldview explanation is compelling—and I believe it is—then conflict and resistance over changes to worship are not only normal but inevitable.[7]

Is it possible that a single service can blend these two approaches? Yes, but the intentionality with which congregational leaders approach the issue may be key. If leaders can't change structure without power relationships being disrupted, they also won't be able to change worship without worldviews clashing. To the degree that worldview differences are both named and negotiated, adding a contemporary service or blending contemporary elements into an existing traditional service is likely to be successfully facilitated.

Several themes are suggested by these theoretical explorations and by analysis of the specific experiences of congregations that changed worship. I offer them as principles for leaders contemplating changes to worship services—especially the addition of a more contemporary service: move slowly, acknowledge losses, and reinforce foundations.

Move Slowly

Worship is the primary cultural expression of a congregation, and changes to it should never be undertaken lightly. Normally a congregation should undertake a six-to-twelve-month inclusive planning process before moving to implementation. Prior to and during the implementation phase, leaders should clarify the rationale for the changes and offer opportunities for members concerned about the changes to articulate their concerns.

Acknowledge Losses

Whether an existing service is transformed or a new service is added, significant losses will be experienced by some in the congregation. In the transition from a traditional worship service to a blended service, senior members might genuinely mourn the absence of beloved hymns, and when a new service is added, all might feel the loss of the "single church" as two functional congregations emerge.

Reinforce Foundations

When a change is made to a congregation's most critical cultural expression—its worship service—members may understandably fear that even deeper beliefs and values might also be at risk. Congregational leaders are well advised to shore up the foundations during these transitions—perhaps by reciting foundational creeds on a more regular basis or by continuing to provide printed bulletins even if the new service is more fluid and less scripted.

Leadership and Change

Leaders have a critical role in dealing with change and conflict in congregational systems, but the role appears to be a reciprocal one. Leaders initiate change and are then held responsible for the outcome of change processes. Certain changes correlate with conflict, and leadership departures correlate with conflict in congregations.[8] When conflict flares, leaders are at greater risk of leaving—in fact, more than twice as likely as in the no-conflict cases.

We have considered two possible explanations for this finding. The first and most obvious is that leaders tend to depart because they mismanage either the change effort or the resulting conflict. I have termed this the "management" explanation. The second, or "symbolic," explanation is that leaders tend to be held responsible for what goes wrong in organizations like congregations, regardless of their actual responsibility. But whether due to mismanagement of change and conflict or simply due to the leader becoming the scapegoat for congregational failures, leaders are at risk of losing their jobs when there is conflict.

Congregational leaders are therefore advised to carefully study the environments in which their congregations are nested and to make adaptive changes that are seen as congruent with the congregation's culture. This study was unable to establish which of the various theories regarding how and why organizations change in response to a changing environment offers the best explanation. A qualitative analysis of respondents' comments reveals support for each of the big three theories—survival of the fittest, survival of the same, and survival of the savvy. It was also apparent that some respondents were keenly aware of their congregation's environment, and others were much less so.

Given the need for organizations to adapt to their changing environments, I hypothesize that leaders who initiate needed change processes to their congregation's structure or culture will in the long run experience more organizational success than leaders who do not. I concur with organizational culture guru Edgar Schein's claim, "Leadership is now the ability to step outside the culture that created the leader and to start evolutionary change processes that are more adaptive."[9] The key is that these processes be truly evolutionary, as revolutionary change tends to be much more disruptive and thus even more vigorously resisted.

Given the tendency of congregations to resist changes to their structure or culture, I also hypothesize that these proactive leaders will experience more conflict than leaders who do not initiate change efforts. This hypothesis is supported by the current study. As we have seen, congregations that initiated changes to their structure or culture were at a higher risk of conflict than those that did not. Successful leaders will thus risk change—and experience more conflict.

Effective leaders will discern not only what needs to be changed in their congregational systems but also how to go about changing it. As congregational researchers Nancy Ammerman and her colleagues coach congregational leaders, leadership involves: (1) "Helping your congregation gain a realistic understanding of its particular situation and circumstances; (2) assisting members to develop a vision for their corporate life that is faithful to their best understanding of God and God's purposes for this congregation in this time and place; and (3) helping them embody that vision in their congregation's corporate life."[10]

The leader's job is thus primarily to name how the congregation's environment is changing and then to initiate a planning and implementation process that responds to those changes out of the core calling and values of that congregation.

Change and Conflict

The change management literature within organizational sociology and management theory is thus instructive for congregational leaders seeking healthy change and growth. While the current research does not provide any magic formulas for church growth, it does demonstrate that certain changes are highly correlated with congregational conflict. Such changes may be inevitable in the life of a healthy congregation, but to the degree that they are anticipated, planned, and communicated, destructive conflict will be diminished.

The key issue underlying successful change efforts may be the quality of the change management process—including the ability to manage the conflict that often results from genuine change efforts. As Carl Dudley and Nancy Ammerman conclude in their research-driven and very practical guide to congregations in transition:

> Perhaps no finding from our study is more commonsensical—and more disturbing—than the discovery that congregations that change are also congregations where there is conflict. People who care about

their congregation will inevitably disagree about how to move forward, so adaptive congregations have found ways of embracing conflict. Discovering that it is possible to disagree but still move forward is one of the critical differences between peaceful-but-stagnant congregations and those that are willing to disturb the status quo.[11]

"Discovering that it is possible to disagree but still move forward is one of the critical differences. . . ." Congregations that succeed at change develop a culture that tolerates if not encourages disagreement. Since leaders shape culture, successful congregations are led by individuals who learn how to disagree respectfully—with each other and with others in the congregation—and invite others to agree or disagree in response. Change-resistant congregations tend to feature leaders who broach no disagreement and thus remain "peaceful but stagnant."

What can the practicing pastor or lay leader learn from this analysis of change and conflict in congregations? I offer the following conclusions:

Conclusion 1: Change is inevitable in religious congregations, and conflict is virtually so. If 45 out of 100 congregations experienced significant conflict in a five-year period, it is reasonable to surmise that the majority would in a ten-year period.

Conclusion 2: What congregations say they fight about (the identified issues) may be less significant than the underlying organizational factors (the systemic issues). Conflict correlates with changes to decision-making structure and worship services, and leadership departures correlate with conflict experiences.

Conclusion 3: Knowing that conflict correlates with structural, cultural, and leadership changes is valuable for leaders, not so that they can avoid making such changes but so that they can prepare for the resistance and conflict that is likely to result. Leaders desiring to avoid destructive conflict will make structural changes slowly and deliberately, and they will introduce cultural changes gently and with substantial communication.

Conclusion 4: Finally, effective congregational leaders will use the tools of their own tradition—including Scripture and ritual—to facilitate the change process. As we saw in Richard McCorry's writing, using the language and familiar stories of the faith community will ease transitions.[12]

According to this study, conflict is most likely to appear when power is threatened or ritual is disrupted. But in congregations, conflict is seldom discussed in such terms. Rather, fights surface over theological issues, like homosexuality, and personnel issues, such as the pastor's performance. The issue of homosexuality does seem to matter at the denominational level, and undoubtedly pastoral performance is a legitimate issue in many congregational disputes.[13] However, this study suggests that what congregational members believe they are most often fighting about—leadership and theology—may not be the actual cause of many congregational disputes. Leadership and theology are visible and thus easy to focus on. Power and ritual are less so. The "battle for the Bible" may be a less significant causal factor for congregational conflict than more human battles—struggles for power and disputes over ritual expressions.

Implications for Congregational Consultants

Conflict is visible—it attracts attention. When conflict surfaces in a congregation, congregational leaders notice. But conflict is useful primarily as a visible symptom of underlying structural dynamics. Consultants who are called to intervene in conflicted congregations, then, should not be concerned primarily with the management of the presenting conflicts.[14] Rather, the goal should be to identify and understand the deeper dynamics within the system that have precipitated the conflict. The objective is to prevent destructive conflict by undertaking proactive change-management efforts and by developing healthy systems rather than merely intervening after a conflict has surfaced.

Despite the well-documented success of mediation for the resolution of interpersonal disputes, congregational conflict consulting has not enjoyed the same high level of success.[15] The two processes are predicated on similar problem-solving steps, so what might account for the difference?

This study points to one possible answer. By accepting the framing of issues offered by the parties to the dispute, some congregational consultants may inadvertently contribute to a misdiagnosis of the underlying causes of the conflict.[16] As we have seen, participants in congregational conflicts tend to explain their conflicts primarily in terms of leadership, theology (especially regarding social issues like homosexuality), personalities, and money. Underlying conflict correlations, however, point to structural and cultural changes as primary factors in congregational conflict. If the real fights are about power and ritual but they are explained in terms of personalities and currently hot issues, the likelihood of successful conflict transformation is diminished.

The process of conflict consulting in congregations, then, will be a reciprocal one. Those who intervene must listen to congregational members and respect members' framing of the critical issues that are in dispute. But the interveners will also need to reframe the identified issues in terms that reflect the systemic nature of the congregation and change dynamics that take place in complex systems. While it is possible that a percentage of congregational conflicts are indeed primarily about homosexuality or personality differences, the majority likely also encompasses systemic patterns and changes to structure or culture.

Conflict is a symptom, but a very useful one. Congregations don't seek assistance until the pain of the presenting symptoms overwhelms their resistance to outside intervention. Congregational consultants who see their primary responsibility as alleviating pain run the risk of perpetuating pathological patterns. If instead they view conflict as a symptom and an opportunity—a symptom of distress in the system but also an opportunity for growth and change within the congregation—they may serve as facilitators of genuine transformation.

The task of the congregational conflict consultant thus becomes one of increasing the organism's capacity to manage its pain while also addressing the underlying source of the distress. Conflict management has a role, as congregational members need tools (such as communication skills) to cope with the higher stress levels. But conflict transformation will be the deeper challenge, as members are given the opportunity to explore the deeper relational patterns in their system—including its responses to change.

Successful resolution, then, will require both the ability to manage the presenting symptoms and the courage to transform deeper patterns. As the Alban Institute's Gil Rendle writes:

> Systems are notoriously adept at colluding around answers that will not make a difference. Congregations faced with an obvious need for change in what they are doing in ministry (e.g., membership is declining) will sometimes remain in a place of denial. . . . So the task of bringing the need for change into a level of consciousness is very important. Effective leaders find the *appropriate* pain and try to keep people there (instead of seeking to solve their perceived problem). The church needs to recover the role of helping people become uncomfortable with their inappropriate behavior.[17]

Again we see that the leader's primary task is one of naming and framing—of bringing "the need for change into a level of consciousness." The temptation will be to avoid naming the elephant in the room—or at least in the environment. Leaders who are successful at change find ways of raising issues and asking questions that make it increasingly impossible for a group to collude in pretending that a given reality does not exist.

Limitations and Future Research

This study suffered from four limitations that I hope can be addressed through future research. First, the research was limited to a population of Presbyterian and Episcopal congregations located primarily in the state of Arizona. Although it provides an accurate glimpse into mainline Protestant congregations in the rapidly growing southwestern United States, future studies of the relationship between change and conflict in congregations should broaden the population to include evangelical and mainline Protestant, Roman Catholic, and Orthodox, and ideally Jewish and Muslim congregations.

Second, this study was unable to establish a causal link between conflict and adding or deleting a worship service. Although the statistical correlation is significant, the fact that I did not request the year of the addition or deletion of a worship service is a significant limitation of this study. Additional quantitative research—designed specifically to explore the causal relationship between conflict and specific types of change in congregations—could address this deficiency.

Third, in each of the 100 congregations included in the sample, I only talked with a single informant—usually the head pastor or priest. While that individual is often the most informed regarding developments in a local congregation, I was unable due to time limitations to confirm his or her impressions and memory by talking with a second informant. Ideally, the study would have been based on information gleaned both from an ordained informant and a lay informant. (Congregational consultants who are asked to intervene in a congregational dispute will typically interview a dozen or more respondents or administer a questionnaire to the entire membership.)

Finally, the correlations between adding or deleting a worship service and conflict, changing structure and conflict, and staff turnover and conflict are all moderate but not extremely strong. Controlling for key demographic variables in a regression model, only adding and deleting a worship service and changing structure retain a significant effect on conflict. A quantitative study including a larger sample of congregations would provide additional statistical power to explore these correlations.

Despite these significant limitations, this research offered or reinforced three significant claims. First, change and conflict are pervasive in religious congregations, even though most changes do not correlate with conflict. Second, the identified issues (what congregations say they fight about) are less significant than underlying structural and systemic issues. Third, the ability to effectively introduce and manage change—in ways consistent with the congregation's own tradition—is a critical skill set for leaders who desire thriving congregations.

Additional research is needed regarding change and conflict in congregations in the major areas noted above. In addition, I would encourage further qualitative research on the critical variable of *leadership* in congregations. Leadership matters, including the ability of leaders to mediate the relationship between the congregation and its environment through well-managed change processes. Despite the surplus of leadership studies in other contexts, relatively little empirical research exists on leadership in congregations. What are the critical leadership skills for introducing change while moderating the resulting resistance and conflict? How can those skills be disseminated to current and future congregational leaders? The findings of research in this area would ideally influence how seminaries prepare pastors for congregational ministry.

Don't Try This Alone

Although the research wasn't able to capture this insight, I am convinced, based on more than twenty years of organizational consulting experience, that leaders have to build a diverse coalition from within the congregation if they want to achieve lasting change. This was modeled by Jesus, who is recorded in all four of the Gospels (Matthew 4, Mark 3, Luke 5, and John 1) calling a diverse group of disciples—ranging from a tax collector collaborating with the Roman regime to a zealot fighting violently to overthrow it. Leaders who want to change their societies (or congregations) start by building a diverse group of change agents who must first learn how to cooperate with each other. (For guidance in forming such a group, please see appendix D. These guidelines can be used either by outside consultants or by internal leaders.)

A charismatic leader may initiate lasting change, but a group that represents the diversity of the community, organization, or society implements it. Congregational leaders who want to change their congregation all by themselves will find to their surprise that congregational culture is far stronger than are they. Congregational leaders who take the time to build a supporting coalition will instead experience change that is both supported and sustainable.

Congregational leaders—clergy and lay—must learn to better manage both change and conflict if congregations are to continue to be relevant to future generations. Congregations have not been immune from the trend of declining participation in voluntary associations. The ability of congregational leaders to monitor their changing environments and to make proactive changes informed by their tradition's values, beliefs, and rituals will be key to future success—if not survival. This book is offered as a modest contribution to that effort.

APPENDIX A

Telephone Survey

Following is the text of a survey administered via phone interviews with 100 congregational leaders. Interview times were scheduled during an initial phone call, and potential respondents were asked if they could commit thirty to forty-five minutes to participating in an interview regarding change and conflict in congregations. During the interview, respondents were first read the disclaimer (below) and then asked if they would consent to being interviewed.

You are being invited to voluntarily participate in a research study regarding change and conflict in congregations. The purpose of the study is to identify possible relationships between growth or decline in congregations and conflict. You are eligible to participate because you are a congregational leader in a Presbyterian or Episcopal congregation in Arizona.

If you agree to participate, your participation will involve participation in one phone survey about your perspective on a variety of issues within your congregation. The survey will take place in a location convenient to you and will last approximately thirty to forty-five minutes. You may choose not to answer some or all of the questions. During the survey, written notes will be made in order to help the investigator review what is said. Your name will not appear on these notes.

Any questions you have will be answered and you may withdraw from the study at any time. There are no known risks from your participation and no direct benefit from your participation is expected. There is no cost to you except for your time, and you will not be compensated.

Only the principal investigator will have access to your name and the information that you provide. In order to maintain your confidentiality, your name will not be revealed in any reports that result from this project. Survey information will be locked in a cabinet in a secure place.

By participating in the survey, you are giving permission for the investigator to use your information for research purposes.

Thank you.

Congregational Demographics

1. What *year* was your congregation founded?

2. What is the average Sunday morning *attendance* at your congregation (all services)?

3. How would you describe the *ethnic* composition of the regular attendees in your congregation, in percentage terms?

    African American ___%
    Asian American ___%
    European American (Anglo) ___%
    Hispanic ___%
    Native American ___%

4. How would you describe the *gender* composition of the regular attendees in your congregation, in percentage terms?

    ___% women and ___% men

5. For how many years have you been pastor of this
    congregation? _____

6. What is the approximate median *age* of those who serve
    on the session or vestry in your congregation?

    __ Under 30
    __ 30–39
    __ 40–49
    __ 50–59
    __ 60–69
    __ 70+

7. What is the annual operating *budget* of your congregation
    for this year (2004)?

8. How would you describe the *community* in which your
    congregation is located?

    __ Rural (unincorporated area)
    __ Suburban (near urban area)
    __ Urban (under 100,000)
    __ Urban (100,000 or more)
    __ Retirement community
    __Other:

Congregational Environment

1. What significant *changes* have taken place in your
    community over the past five years that might have
    affected your congregation? Check category or categories:

__ Population growth/decline
__ Increase/decrease in ethnic diversity
__ Increase/decrease in employment opportunities
__ Improvement/decline in school system
__ Improvement/decline in health care system
__ Other:

2.   What changes have you seen in terms of *other* Christian
     congregations coming into or expanding in your community?
     Check category or categories:

     __ Significant expansion
     __ Some expansion
     __ No change
     __ Some decline
     __ Significant decline
     __Other:

3.   What organizations *outside* of your church have had the
     most impact on your congregation the last five years?
     Rank from 1 (high impact) to 5 (low impact).

     __ National denomination
     __ Regional presbytery or diocese
     __ Local association of churches
     __ Influential congregation (for example, Willow Creek)
     __ Other (describe):

Congregational Structure

1.   Please rank the respective influence of these different
     groups and individuals on decision making in your
     congregation. Indicate at least the most influential and
     second most influential groups or individuals. Where are
     the important *financial* decisions in your congregation
     made?

     _____ Congregational meetings
     _____ Pastor
     _____ Vestry or Session
     _____ Committees or Teams
     _____ Other (describe):

2.   Where are the important *staffing* decisions in your
     congregation made? (Rank)

     _____ Congregational meetings
     _____ Pastor
     _____ Vestry or Session
     _____ Committees or Teams
     _____ Other (describe):

3.   Where are the important decisions about *worship* made
     in your congregation? (Rank)

     _____ Congregational meetings
     _____ Pastor
     _____ Vestry or Session
     _____ Committees or Teams
     _____ Other (describe):

4. Where are the important decisions about *buildings* made
    in your congregation? (Rank)

    _____ Congregational meetings
    _____ Pastor
    _____ Vestry or Session
    _____ Committees or Teams
    _____ Other (describe):

5. In general, where would you say the real power lies in
    your congregation? (Rank)

    _____ Congregational meetings
    _____ Pastor
    _____ Vestry or Session
    _____ Committees or Teams
    _____ Other (describe):

6. Is there a formal *flow chart* that shows lines of
    accountability in the congregation?

    __Yes   __No   __Don't know

7. Are there written *job descriptions* for church staff
    describing their roles and to whom they report?

    __Yes   __No   __Don't know

8. Does the congregation have formal *rules and procedures*
    to govern any of the following:

    __ Personnel policy
    __ Financial management
    __ Office procedures

__ Grievance procedures
__ No written rules or procedures

Congregational Culture

1. What *percentage* of your congregation's regular attendees
    (adults only) would participate in the following activities
    in a given week:

    ___ % Sunday school classes
    ___ % Sunday or Wednesday evening meetings
    ___ % Small groups
    ___ % Committee or session/vestry meetings
    ___ % Other (describe):

2. Where would you place your congregation in terms of its
    primary identification with your denomination and your
    community (on a 1–5 continuum)?

    ___ Only denomination
    ___ Mostly denomination
    ___ Both denomination and community
    ___ Mostly community
    ___ Only community

3. What are some specific examples of how your congregation
    participates in *denominational/diocesan/presbytery* activities?
    Check category or categories:

    __ Attend presbytery/diocesan meetings
    __ Contribute to denominational causes
    __ Serve on diocesan/presbytery committees

__ No involvement
__ Other:

4. What are some specific examples of how your
    congregation participates in *community* activities? Check
    category or categories:

    __ Sponsor community/neighborhood events
    __ Permit community groups to use facility
    __ Provide community services (for example, soup
        kitchen, clothing distribution)
    __ No involvement
    __ Other

Congregational Change

1. What changes have you seen in your congregation the last
    five years? Check category or categories:

    __ Pastoral/staff turnover
    __ Congregational growth/decline
    __ Added/deleted a service
    __ New building project
    __ New program within congregation
    __ New community outreach
    __ Other:

2. How many salaried, full-time *staff*, including the pastor,
    are there in your congregation today? ___ How many
    were there in each of the following years?

    2004 ___
    2003 ___

2002 ___
2001 ___
2000 ___

3. If there were *changes in staffing* in the last five years,
    please describe what kind of change(s) occurred and the
    year(s) that the change(s) took place.

    __ 2004 (Change: _____)
    __ 2003 (Change: _____)
    __ 2002 (Change: _____)
    __ 2001 (Change: _____)
    __ 2000 (Change: _____)

4. If there were changes in *Sunday morning attendance* the
    last five years, please describe the nature of the change(s)
    and the year(s) that the change(s) took place.

    __ 2004 (Change: _____)
    __ 2003 (Change: _____)
    __ 2002 (Change: _____)
    __ 2001 (Change: _____)
    __ 2000 (Change: _____)

5. Over the past five years (since 2000), how many
    new members would you estimate have joined your
    congregation? _____

6. If new members have joined your congregation in the last
    five years, please describe how the *new members might be
    similar to or differ from* the longer tenured members.

Possible probes: Ethnicity, age, education level, theology, worship preferences

7. Over the past five years (since 2000), how many existing members would you estimate left your congregation, for whatever reason? _____

8. If some members left your congregation in the last five years, please describe how the *old members who left might be similar to or differ from* your current members.

    Possible probes: Ethnicity, age, education level, theology, worship preferences

9. If there were changes in *decision-making patterns* in your congregation the last five years, please describe the nature of the change(s) and the year(s) that the change took place. Check category or categories:

    __ 2004 (Change: _____) __ More congregational meetings
    __ 2003 (Change: _____) __ Fewer congregational meetings
    __ 2002 (Change: _____) __ More session/vestry meetings
    __ 2001 (Change: _____) __ Fewer session/vestry meetings
    __ 2000 (Change: _____) __ Other:

10. If there were changes in the *fellowship patterns* in your congregation the last five years, please describe the nature of the change(s) and the year(s) that the change took place. Check category or categories:

    __ 2004 (Change: _____) __ More potluck suppers
    __ 2003 (Change: _____) __ Fewer potluck suppers
    __ 2002 (Change: _____) __ More small fellowship groups

__ 2001 (Change: _____) __ Fewer small fellowship groups
__ 2000 (Change: _____) __ Other:

Congregational Conflict

1. In the last five years, has your congregation experienced a *conflict* significant enough to convene a special meeting or call in outside help?

    __Yes   __ No __ Don't know

2. If yes, can you identify the *year(s)* that the conflict(s) occurred?

    __ 2004
    __ 2003
    __ 2002
    __ 2001
    __ 2000

3. On a scale of 1 to 5, according to the descriptions below, how would you rank the intensity of the *most recent* conflict?

    __ Problem resolved/no relationships damaged (1)
    __ Difficult disagreement/relationships strained (2)
    __ Challenging conflict/relationships damaged (3)
    __ Major fight/individuals or families left (4)
    __ Irreconcilable differences/split/schism (5)

    (Note: Numbers 1–5 in parentheses correspond to Speed Leas's Levels of Conflict)

4. In the most recent conflict, who were the *principals* in the conflict? Check category or categories:

    __ Key families/individuals
    __ Pastor/other staff
    __ Vestry/session members
    __ Committee/team leaders
    __ Other:

5. In the most recent conflict, what were the issues in dispute? Check category or categories:

    __ Personality differences
    __ Leadership style
    __ Buildings
    __ Finances
    __ New members versus old members
    __ Moral failure by someone in leadership
    __ Generational differences
    __ Other:

6. In the most recent conflict, what was the *outcome* of the conflict? Check category or categories:

    __ Pastor/staff left
    __ Members left
    __ Issues resolved without major losses
    __ Relationships damaged but no departures
    __ New procedures/structure developed
    __ Other:

7.   On a scale of 1 to 5, according to the descriptions below,
     how would you rank the intensity of the *next most recent*
     conflict?

     __ Problem resolved/no relationships damaged (1)
     __ Difficult disagreement/relationships strained (2)
     __ Challenging conflict/relationships damaged (3)
     __ Major fight/individuals or families left (4)
     __ Irreconcilable differences/split/schism (5)

     (Note: Numbers 1–5 in parentheses correspond to Speed
     Leas's Levels of Conflict)

8.   In the next most recent conflict, who were the *principals*
     in the conflict? Check category or categories:

     __ Key families/individuals
     __ Pastor/other staff
     __ Vestry/session members
     __ Committee/team leaders
     __ Other:

9.   In the next most recent conflict, what were the *issues* in
     dispute? Check category or categories:

     __ Personality differences
     __ Leadership style
     __ Buildings
     __ Finances
     __ New members versus old members
     __ Moral failure by someone in leadership
     __ Generational differences
     __ Other:

10. In the next most recent conflict, what was the *outcome* of the conflict? Check category or categories:

___ Pastor/staff left
___ Members left
___ Issues resolved without major losses
___ Relationships damaged but no departures
___ New procedures/structure developed
___ Other:

Other

1. What trends or developments make you most *hopeful* about the future of your congregation?

2. Is there *anything else* you would like to say about your congregation that would help me more fully understand it?

APPENDIX B

Correlations between Conflict and Key Independent Variables

VARIABLE

1	2	3	4	5	6	7	8	9	10

1. Conflict (n=97)

1.0

2. Denomination (n=100)

−.007 1.0

3. Age (n=100)

−.038 −.099 1.0

4. Size (n=100)

.146 −.060 .207* 1.0

5. Pastoral tenure (n=100)

−.183 .002 −.026 .302** 1.0

6. Staff change (n= 100)

.312** −.132 .194 .305** −.330** 1.0

7. Worship change (n=100)

.292** −.023 .227* .284** −.070 .398** 1.0

8. Building project (n=100)

.069   .010   .102   .196   .195   .092   .075   1.0

---

9. Size transition (n=100)

−.014   −.039   .060   −.109   −.189   .128   .208*   −.004   1.0

---

10. Decision change (n=100)

.377*** −.143   −.107   .109   −.294** .241*   .164   −.012   −.029   1.0

---

11. Fellowship change (n=98)

.221*   .028   .093   .161   .000   .129   .234*   .158   −.007   .412***

---

*p<.05

** p< 0.01

***p<.0001

p = probability

APPENDIX C

Logistic Regression— Full Model

Case Processing Summary

Unweighted Cases (a)		N	Percent	
Selected Cases	Included in Analysis	93	93.0	
	Missing Cases	7	7.0	
	Total	100	100.0	
Unselected Cases		0	.0	
Total		100	100.0	

a. If weight is in effect, see classification table for the total number of cases.

Omnibus Tests of Model Coefficients

		Chi-square	Df	Sig.	
Step 1	Step	23.825	9	.005	
	Block	23.825	9	.005	
	Model	23.825	9	.005	

Model Summary

Step	– 2 Log likelihood	Cox & Snell R Square	Nagelkerke R Square
1	104.831(a)	.226	.302

a. Estimation terminated at iteration number 5 because parameter estimates changed by less than .001.

Classification Table (a)

Observed	Predicted					
	Conflict	Percentage Correct				
	0	1				
Step 1	Conflict	0		36	13	73.5
		1		14	30	68.2
	Overall Percentage				71.0	

a. The cut value is .500

Variables in the Equation

		B	S.E.	Wald	Df.	Sig	Exp (B)
Step 1(a)	Denomination	.076	.505	.023	1	.880	1.079
	Date of Founding	−.009	.008	1.232	1	.267	.991
	Tenure of Pastor	−.043	.046	.867	1	.352	.958
	Attendance in 2000	.001	.001	.703	1	.402	1.001
	Pastor/Staff Turnover	.872	.687	1.611	1	.204	2.391
	Added/Deleted a Worship Service	1.186	.545	4.729	1	.030	3.272
	New Building Project	.201	.509	.156	1	.693	1.223
	Size Transition	−.101	.625	.026	1	.871	.904
	Decision Change	1.193	.571	4.366	1	.037	3.296
	Constant	16.095	15.877	1.028	1	.311	9774703.548

a. Variable(s) entered on step 1: Denomination, Date of Founding, Tenure of Pastor, Attendance in 2000, Pastor/Staff Turnover, Added/Deleted Worship Service, New Building Project, Size Transition, Decision Change.

APPENDIX D

Forming a Reference Committee in Congregational Change or Conflict

When I first begin working with conflicted congregations in 1987, I approached my initial cases in the role of a mediator. I soon discovered that the skills of listening and reframing that had served me so well in interpersonal mediation sessions were inadequate to address the scope and intensity of these complex multiparty cases. In 1989 I attended an Alban Institute course titled "Consulting with Severely Conflicted Churches" led by Speed Leas. With the new hat of "conflict consultant," I now approached congregational conflict with a diagnostic and treatment model, producing countless pages of surveys, analysis, and recommendations.

In follow-up evaluations, I soon realized that my recommendations were often perused but seldom implemented. The problem seemed to be that my recommendations were, well, *mine*. Clients clearly appreciated the depth of my involvement in their cases and the breadth of my understanding of the issues, but they had had no investment in developing the process or the recommendations. Thus, they possessed no stake in the implementation of the recommendations. Like so many reports, mine sat on the shelf, and little change occurred within the system itself.

147

By 1992, I realized that another model was needed. I began to request that the governing bodies of the conflicted congregations with which I was asked to work appoint a "Reference Committee" to assist me in designing an intervention process and in developing recommendations.

Purpose of a Reference Committee

In sociological literature, a "reference group" is the immediate social group that provides an individual member with the sense of the norms and values that are important in the larger group. The purpose of a Reference Committee (or, in some systems, Reference Team) is to accompany the outside consultant(s) in the process of designing and implementing a systemic change process. Ideally, therefore, Reference Committee members should be involved in the data gathering and assessment stages of the intervention process. When that is not possible, Reference Committee members can be included in the process of analyzing data collected by the consultant and developing appropriate recommendations for an ongoing process.

Composition of the Reference Committee

An ideal Reference Committee is composed of five to seven members chosen to represent the diversity of the congregation. Most Reference Committees I have worked with included a balance of men and women, younger and older members, diverse perspectives on the issues in dispute, and, where it existed in the congregation, ethnic diversity. Reference Committees are generally appointed by the governing body of the congregation, with the understanding that they are to serve as an ad hoc committee or task force.

Training the Committee

Reference Committee members require training to understand that their essential job is to advocate a fair process and not a particular outcome. Given that Reference Committees generally represent the spectrum of views in the congregation, some members may be reluctant to place a commitment to process ahead of their desire for a particular outcome. Thus the consultant's job is to ensure that roles are clarified on an ongoing basis, not just at the initial meeting. Also, the quality of the dialogue among Reference Committee members tends to affect the quality of the overall dialogue within the congregation. Therefore, consultants may also need to provide training in cooperative communication skills to committee members and to develop and enforce guidelines for discussion, or ground rules.

Appointment Process

In most situations, an external conflict consultant initially contracts with the governing board of a congregation. As part of the contract (or memorandum of understanding, if such is preferred), the consultant should clarify her or his intent to work with a Reference Committee as well as the governing board's responsibility to appoint one. Guidelines for appointing a Reference Committee can be provided to or discussed with the governing board. Prospective committee members should be informed that their service could be required for anywhere from six to twelve months and that their role in developing recommendations could mean that some or many in the congregation might be unhappy with parts of the outcome, and thus with them.

When Not to Appoint

A Reference Committee need not be appointed when the conflict
is not systemwide or when the existing leadership group is functioning well enough to oversee the intervention process. These
two conditions are unlikely in a higher-level conflict but may often be present in Level 3 or lower conflicts (on the Leas scale).
Clearly, one of the first tasks of the outside consultant(s) is to assess not only the intensity but also the breadth of the congregational conflict. Such an initial assessment should occur prior to
the systemwide assessment that is often characterized by written
surveys, focus group interviews, and so forth.

Benefits and Dangers

The primary value of working with a Reference Committee is that
both the intervention process and the resulting recommendations tend to be "owned" by the diverse group of congregational
members who participated on the committee. Written evaluations
following such interventions have shown generally higher satisfaction rates than comparable cases where I had not used Reference
Committees. The main danger that should be mentioned is that
in very high intensity conflict (upper Level 4 or Level 5), Reference Committee members may pay a personal price when the inevitable losses that accompany such conflicts occur. Despite their
best efforts, consultants and committee members will be unable
to eliminate the natural personal and organizational consequences
of these conflicts and may be blamed by some members of the
congregation for their inability to work miracles.

Notes

Preface

1. In a "history boarding" process, the facilitator leads a congregation through a discussion of various stages of its organizational history, beginning with the founding period and proceeding through to the present. The congregation will often recall and identify the stages by the successive senior pastors who led the congregation throughout its history, and the facilitator will encourage discussion of both joyous memories and painful ones in each stage. History boarding is a remarkably effective way to assist a congregation in noticing and naming patterns that have developed over time.

Introduction
More than a Family System

1. Few subjects are as contested in the sociology of religion literature as that of participation rates. While about 40 percent of U.S. residents consistently tell pollsters they have attended a religious service "in the last seven days," actual attendance rates are likely much closer to 20 percent on any given weekend. See C. Kirk Hadaway

and Penny Long Marler, "How Many Americans Attend Worship Each Week? An Alternative Approach to Measurement," *Journal for the Scientific Study of Religion* 44, no. 3 (2005): 307–22.

2. Robert D. Putnam, *Bowling Alone: The Collapse and Revival of American Community* (New York: Simon and Schuster, 2000), 66.

3. Mark Chaves et al., "The National Congregations Study: Background, Methods and Selected Results," *Journal for the Scientific Study of Religion* 38, no. 4:458–76.

4. The FACT study, conducted in 2000 by the Hartford Institute for Religious Research, surveyed more than 14,000 U.S. congregations. The results were published in March 2001. Findings are available through Hartford Seminary at the Faith Communities Today (FACT) Web site: http://fact.hartsem.edu/. Jack Marcum's research appeared in 2001 in his "Monday Morning" newsletter and can be found at www.pcusa.org/research/monday/conflict.htm.

5. Surprisingly, one of the least likely causes of conflict reported by the 541 Presbyterian congregations that responded to the FACT study was theology. The well-publicized struggles over homosexuality, for example, seem to take place primarily at the regional (judicatory) and denominational levels rather than within local congregations.

6. Roy W. Pneuman, "Nine Common Sources of Conflict in Churches," *When the Conflict Is in My Congregation* (2001), Thomas Jefferson District of the UUA, http://uua.org/tjd/resources.

7. Many books have been written applying family systems theory to congregational life, most notably *Generation to Generation: Family Process in Church and Synagogue* by Edwin H. Friedman (New York: Guilford Press, 1985).

8.   Larry E. Greiner, "Evolution and Revolution as Organizations Grow," *Harvard Business Review* 15, no. 4 (1972).

9.   A size transition occurs when a congregation moves up or down from its current size to a new size. For example, a congregation could transition from pastoral size past the 200 barrier to become program size, or it could decline the other direction.

10. Edgar Schein, *Organizational Culture and Leadership,* 3rd ed. (San Francisco: Jossey-Bass, 2004), 17.

11. Lisa Schirch, *Ritual and Symbol in Peacebuilding* (Bloomfield, CT: Kumarian Press, 2005), 2, 3.

12. Jeffrey Pfeffer and Gerald R. Salancik, *The External Control of Organizations: A Resource Dependence Perspective* (Stanford, CA: Stanford University Press, 2003), 17.

13. Ibid.

14. Friedman, *Generation to Generation,* 218.

15. Nancy Tatom Ammerman, *Congregation and Community* (New Brunswick, NJ: Rutgers University Press, 1997).

16. Paul J. DiMaggio and Walter W. Powell, "The Iron Cage Revisited: Institutional Isomorphism and Collective Rationality in Organizational Fields," *American Sociological Review* 48, no. 2 (April 1983): 147–60.

17. Robert Wuthnow, *The Restructuring of American Religion: Society and Faith since World War II* (Princeton, NJ: Princeton University Press, 1988); Mark Chaves, "Secularization as Declining Religious Authority," *Social Forces* 72, no. 3 (March 1994): 749–74; and Amanda Porterfield, *The Transformation of American Religion: The Story of a Late Twentieth-Century Awakening* (New York: Oxford University Press, 2001).

18. DiMaggio and Powell, "The Iron Cage Revisited," 149.

19. Lynn Anderson, *Navigating the Winds of Change: How to Manage Change in the Church* (West Monroe, LA: Howard Publishing Company, 1994); Gilbert R. Rendle, *Leading Change in the Congregation: Spiritual and Organizational Tools for Leaders* (Herndon, VA: Alban Institute, 1998); and Mary K. Sellon, Daniel Smith, and Gail F. Grossman, *Redeveloping the Congregation: A How-to for Lasting Change* (Herndon, VA: Alban Institute, 2002).

20. This change model is drawn from the work of the Harvard Business School's John Kotter, author of the very influential book *Leading Change*. A summary of his eight-step model can be found in John P. Kotter and Dan S. Cohen, *The Heart of Change: Real-life Stories of How People Change Their Organizations* (Boston: Harvard Business Press, 2002).

21. Georg Simmel, *Conflict* (New York: Free Press, 1955), 43; Dean R. Hoge, *Division in the Protestant House: The Basic Reasons behind Intra-Church Conflicts* (Philadelphia: Westminster, 1976); and Hugh F. Halverstadt, *Managing Church Conflict* (Louisville: Westminster John Knox Press, 1991).

22. Fred Kniss, *Disquiet in the Land: Cultural Conflict in American Mennonite Communities* (New Brunswick, NJ: Rutgers University Press, 1997).

23. Mary Lou Steed, "Church Schism and Secession: A Necessary Sequence?" *Review of Religious Research* 27, no. 4 (June 1986): 344–55.

Chapter 1
Overview of the Study

1. For a thoughtful example of what causes congregational conflict, see Peter Steinke's list of "Thirteen Triggers of

Anxiety for Congregations," in Peter L. Steinke, *Congregational Leadership in Anxious Times: Being Calm and Courageous No Matter What* (Herndon, VA: Alban Institute, 2006).

2.   Access through "gatekeepers" is critical in many research projects involving human participants. Once researchers identify a population they wish to study, they often have to secure permission from institutional leaders to carry out the proposed research.

3.   I originally proposed a much smaller sample size of 25 to my dissertation committee, which urged that I increase the sample size to at least 100 congregations. Although it requires considerably more time to survey 100 congregations, a sample size of 100 or more cases results in more statistical power—a greater likelihood of obtaining statistically significant results.

4.   "Nonresponse" was a much more significant reason for nonparticipation than was outright refusal. Only three pastors or priests told me directly that they did not wish to participate in the survey, but a much higher number failed to return my calls. Overall, I had a 70 percent response rate, meaning that 30 percent of congregations in the population did not participate in the study. Perhaps this preference to avoid contact rather than directly decline provides an additional clue to conflict management strategies in this population of congregations.

5.   The *mean* of a group of numbers is the mathematical average, whereas the *median* represents the midpoint when the all congregational attendance figures are arranged from lowest to highest. According to Webster's the median is "a value in an ordered set of values below and above which there is an equal number of values or which is the arithmetical mean of the two middle numbers if there is no one middle number." The mean attendance is higher than the median in most surveys

of congregations as a few large congregations tend to increase the average attendance number, even though most congregations are in fact rather small.

6. These are higher thresholds than the ones originally proposed by Arlin Rothauge, who placed the breakpoints at 50, 150, and 350. However, my own experience has been that congregations can function as family size at up to 75 in average year-round attendance, and as pastoral size at up to 200. The threshold for transitioning from pastoral size to program size is harder to discern, but based on my experience with congregations in conflict, congregations up to 400 in average attendance are more pastor focused than program focused.

7. A recent national survey found the gender proportion in U.S. congregations to be 61 percent female and 39 percent male, indicating that this sample may approximate national averages—at least in terms of gender balance. Cynthia Woolever and Deborah Bruce, *A Field Guide to U.S. Congregations: Who's Going Where and Why* (Louisville, KY: Westminster John Knox, 2002).

8. This mean is higher than the four to six years of median tenure found in the National Congregations Survey, although the median tenure in my study was also six years. The NCS measured median tenure both from the "congregations' perspective" (yielding the lower number) and the "attenders' perspective" (yielding the higher number).

9. Chaves, *Congregations in America*, 223.

10. Ten of the Episcopalian respondents explained membership losses by referencing the "Robinson effect," the impact of the very public conflict over the ordination as bishop of Gene Robinson, an openly gay bishop, in the Diocese of New Hampshire in 2003.

11. I am using Rothauge's typology of family-size, pastoral-size, program-size, and corporate-size congregations, with break points revised and placed at 75, 200, and 400 average year-round attendance. See Arlin J. Rothauge, *Sizing Up a Congregation for New Member Ministry* (New York: Episcopal Church Center, 1983).

12. This is strikingly consistent with Peter Steinke's estimate that "about four out of ten congregations in any five-year period [will] face a moderate to serious conflict," *Congregational Leadership in Anxious Times*, 101.

13. "Conflict intensity" was measured on a scale developed by Speed Leas of the Alban Institute. It ranges from a low of 1, signifying a "problem to solve," to a high of 5, signifying an "intractable situation." Most congregations do not report that they are experiencing a conflict until it moves beyond Level 2 ("disagreement") to Level 3 ("contest") or even Level 4 ("fight or flight"). After hearing descriptions of each of these five levels, respondents in my survey were asked to indicate the level of the conflict they were describing.

14. Staff departures nearly doubled in cases where respondents reported a second conflict during the five-year reporting period. Of the 10 congregations that experienced a second conflict, 6 (60 percent) also reported that a pastor or member of the staff left as a result of the conflict.

15. Only 5 of the 45 respondents from conflicted congregations explicitly mentioned intervention by an outside consultant not linked with their judicatory.

16. I determined growth simply by comparing reported attendance in the earliest requested reporting period (2000) to attendance in the most recent reporting period (2004). Congregations that reported a decline or showed no numerical increases were coded "no growth," whereas

congregations that increased by at least one member over the five-year period were coded as growing.

17. Information about a mission statement was not requested on the survey. However, a research assistant searched for websites for all 100 congregations in the sample and identified 52 congregations that had a written and posted mission statement.

18. Perhaps family-size congregations tended to be conflict averse because of the single-cell nature of the organism and the cultural emphasis on unity and harmony. Or perhaps it is simply due to the reality that family-size congregations contain fewer people and programs than do the other sizes—and thus there is less to fight about.

19. Statistical significance is the degree to which a value is greater or smaller than would be expected by chance. It does not mean the finding is important, only that it is reliable. Significance allows researchers to say how confident they are that a particular relationship exists, and is expressed in percentage terms. When the percentage is very low (for example, .001 level), it suggests that we have a high level of confidence the relationship is not due to randomness. Percentages up to .05 are generally considered significant.

20. A dummy variable is a variable the researcher creates from existing data to represent a certain phenomenon. In this case, congregations that experienced a size transition (up or down) were coded "1" (to represent that a transition had occurred), and congregations that did not experience a size transition were coded "0" (for no transition). When included in the regression model, the dummy variable serves to indicate if there is a correlation between the size transition occurring and the presence of conflict.

21. Of the 100 congregations in the sample, 43 experienced turnover at the level of lead or senior pastor during the five-year period requested by the survey.

22. The total number of issues is greater than the total number of conflict incidents because some respondents cited two or more issues involved in the conflict.

Chapter 2
Structure and Power

1. Friedman, *Generation to Generation.*

2. David Knoke, *Organizing for Political Action: The Political Economies of Associations* (New York: Gruyter, 1990), 12.

3. Max Weber, "Bureaucracy," in *From Max Weber: Essays in Sociology* (New York: Oxford University Press, 1946).

4. Pneuman, "Nine Common Sources of Conflict in Churches."

5. Alice Mann, *The In-Between Church: Navigating Size Transitions in Congregations* (Herndon, VA: Alban Institute, 1998).

6. Ammerman, *Congregation and Community,* 333.

7. Of the 14 remaining cases of structural change, 4 each occurred in family-size and corporate-size congregations and another 6 in program-size congregations.

8. Of the 46 congregations that initiated a building project during the five-year period of the study, 50 percent experienced a conflict, compared to those that did not build and experienced conflict at a 43 percent rate. The difference, however, is not statistically significant, as neither figure varies significantly from the overall conflict rate of 45 percent.

9.   Israel Galindo, *The Hidden Lives of Congregations: Discerning Church Dynamics* (Herndon, VA: Alban Institute, 2004).

10. As a congregation matures, just like an individual, its patterns and habits become more firmly entrenched. To say that a "congregation's homeostasis becomes stronger" as it matures is simply to note that the older a congregation the more the patterns and habits become well established.

11. Charles C. Manz and Henry P. Sims, *Business without Bosses: How Self-Managing Teams Are Building High-Performance Companies* (New York: John Wiley and Sons, 1995).

12. Controlling for key demographic variables such as the age and size of the congregation, those congregations that changed their decision-making structure were about 3.3 times more likely to experience conflict than those that did not.

13. Rosabeth Moss Kanter, *Men and Women of the Corporation* (Jackson, TN: Basic Books, 1977), 174.

14. Ibid., 178.

15. Ibid., 190.

16. Larry E. Greiner and Virginia E. Schein, *Power and Organization Development: Mobilizing Power to Implement Change* (Reading, MA: Addison-Wesley, 1988), 20.

17. I wrote on this subject in the early 1990s, when lack of awareness of power imbalances in religious organizations was particularly acute. Since that time many denominations have undertaken clergy awareness programs regarding issues of professional boundaries and power. From my one hundred conversations with pastors in Arizona and New Mexico in 2004–2005, however, it appears that power continues to be an uncomfortable topic for many ordained congregational leaders.

18. *Mimetic isomorphism*, a term coined by organizational sociologists Walter Powell and Paul DiMaggio, refers to the process by which organizations subconsciously become more and more like their peers, particularly the ones perceived to be most successful. The Israelites desired a king, as the neighboring tribes had, despite the fact that God clearly preferred they be led by spiritual prophets.

19. This story, recorded in Acts 6:1–7, is so rich that I will again refer to it in chapter 5.

20. The conflict between Cephas (Peter) and Paul, recorded by Paul in Galatians 2, is a classic illustration of the maxim that most conflicts have multiple causes. This appears to be a case where two very strong-willed men (a personality conflict) butted heads over whether or not Gentile believers had to obey the Jewish law (a contested theological issue), all in the absence of a clear decision-making structure (a lack of role definition for the principal parties).

Chapter 3
Worship—the Primary Expression
of a Congregation's Culture

1. Chaves et al., "National Congregations Study."

2. Ammerman, *Congregation and Community*; Penny Edgell Becker, *Congregations in Conflict: Cultural Models of Local Religious Life* (New York: Cambridge University Press, 1999).

3. Carl S. Dudley and David A. Roozen, "Faith Communities Today: A Report on Religion in the United States Today," Hartford Institute for Religion Research, Hartford Seminary, 2001, http://fact.hartsem.edu/Final%20FACTrpt.pdf.

4. Chaves et al., "National Congregations Study."

5. Ronald P. Byars, *The Future of Protestant Worship: Beyond the Worship Wars* (Louisville: Westminster John Knox, 2002).

6. When only those congregations that added a worship service are considered, the odds ratio in the logistic regression model drops to 1.8, and the effect on conflict is not significant at the .05 level. This means that statistically significant correlation with conflict holds only for adding or dropping a service, not for specifically adding a service.

7. There was not a statistically significant correlation between declining attendance and dropping a worship service, but one would not be expected given the very small number of cases (nine).

8. Margaret Mead, "Ritual and Social Crisis," in the *Roots of Ritual*, ed. James D. Shaughnessy (Grand Rapids, MI: Eerdmans, 1972), quoted in Schirch, *Ritual and Symbol in Peacebuilding*.

9. Willow Creek is a megachurch in the Chicago area.

10. One of the more visible symbols of resistance to praise music at one of the congregations in the sample was that some older members who disliked such music refused to stand or sing when "off the wall" songs—song lyrics projected on a screen— were sung by the congregation. This form of passive resistance to the innovation did not deter its adoption, but it did enhance the perception of conflict over the introduction of praise music.

11. A "change to worship" consisted of adding a worship service, deleting a worship service, or both adding and deleting a worship service (sometimes by replacing one service with another) for other than seasonal reasons during the five-year period covered by the study.

12. Becker, *Congregations in Conflict*, 323.

13. As noted earlier, no claims can be made about the causal direction of this relationship, as dates were requested only for the conflict experience, not for the change to worship. It is significant, however, that all but five of the congregations making a change to worship were adding a service (not a likely event after a conflict experience), and that many of those respondents volunteered that it was a "contemporary service."

14. Mark Chaves, *Congregations in America* (Cambridge, MA: Harvard University Press, 2004), 127.

15. Weber, "Bureaucracy."

16. Congregations that reported two or three significant changes in their environment were 17 percent more likely to add a worship service than congregations that reported no changes or only one significant change in their environment. At the same time, larger congregations (more than 200 in average attendance) were less likely to be in very dynamic environments than were smaller congregations (below 200 in average attendance).

17. Schirch, *Ritual and Symbol in Peacebuilding*, 17.

18. Eric Bertish, "Ritual and Conflict," posting to In Nominee-list, March 22, 2003, http://mail.sjgames.com/pipermail/in-nominee-list. Accessed June 14, 2006.

19. Shane Hipps, *The Hidden Power of Electronic Culture: How Media Shapes Faith, the Gospel, and Church* (Grand Rapids, MI: Zondervan, 2005), 153.

20. Alice Mann, "What Happens Between Sizes? Why Congregations Get Stuck," in *Size Transitions in Congregations*, ed. Beth Ann Gaede (Herdon, VA: Alban Institute, 2001), 48.

21. "Good Order in Worship" is how Today's New International Version titles the section of 1 Corinthians 14:26–40.

22. Research participants were asked only if their congregation added or deleted a worship service during the previous five years for "other than seasonal reasons." However, many respondents who reported adding a worship service volunteered that it was a "contemporary service." A "qualitative analysis" means that this theme was identified by summarizing respondent comments in response to this question about adding a worship service.

23. The "disruption of group cohesion" hypothesis was less supported because conflict occurred in larger congregations that introduced a new worship service at a slightly higher rate than it occurred in smaller congregations that did so. Group cohesion is presumed to be more important in smaller (fewer than 200 in regular attendance) congregations, which are viewed as single-cell organisms.

Chapter 4
Leadership in Congregations

1. "Tsunamic Catastrophe: 'Let my Heart Be Broken . . . ,'" Christianity Today.com, http://www.christianitytoday .com/ch/news/2005/jan27.html.

2. Lead pastors may not even be aware of all that goes on in their congregational systems, particularly in larger congregations. Nonetheless, they are held responsible for developments within the congregation.

3. Jim Collins, *Good to Great: Why Some Companies Make the Leap . . . and Others Don't* (New York: Harper Business, 2001).

4. Stephen J. Zaccaro and Richard J. Klimoski, eds., *The Nature of Organizational Leadership: Understanding the Performance Imperatives Confronting Today's Leaders* (San Francisco: Pfeiffer and Company, 2001).

5. Ibid., 10.
6. Ibid., 13.
7. In the simplistic but memorable phrase that I teach students in my organizational classes, successful leaders will strive to "know yourself, know your organization, and know your environment."
8. The Pearson correlation for decision changes with a pastor/staff change is .241. The Pearson correlation for a change in worship with a pastor/staff change is .398. Both of these correlations are statistically significant, suggesting that the association of turnover with these changes to structure and worship are not random occurrences.
9. Larger congregations have a greater likelihood of staff turnover during a five-year period for the simple reason that there are more staff positions in which turnover can occur.
10. During the five-year reporting period, staff turnover occurred in 89 percent of the 45 conflict cases, whereas in only 62 percent of the 52 nonconflict cases did staff turnover occur. (In three of the cases respondents did not know if a conflict had occurred during the previous five years.)
11. The "party of the Pharisees" apparently consisted of those believers who had held leadership positions in the Jewish religious system that prevailed in Judea and who believed that discipleship needed to include keeping all aspects of the Jewish law, including circumcision. Although Paul himself was educated as a Pharisee, he had concluded that strict adherence to Mosaic Law was no longer needed. (See Romans 7 and 8.)
12. Sections of this chapter were adapted from *The Little Book of Healthy Organizations,* coauthored by David Brubaker and Ruth Zimmerman (Intercourse, PA: Good Books, forthcoming).

Chapter 5
Change and Conflict

1. DiMaggio and Powell, "Iron Cage Revisited."
2. Ammerman, *Congregation and Community*.
3. Of the 46 congregations that initiated a building project during the five-year period of the study, 50 percent experienced a conflict, compared to those that did not build and experienced conflict at a 43 percent rate. The difference, however, is not statistically significant, as neither figure varies significantly from the overall conflict rate of 45 percent.
4. Pneuman, "Nine Common Sources of Conflict in Churches."
5. D. M. Schneider and C. Goldwasser, "Be a Model Leader of Change," *Management Review* 87, no. 3 (1998): 41–45.
6. According to the book *The Quote Verifier* by Ralph Keyes (2006), this quotation cannot be traced to a published source. However, Keyes notes that the Official Mahatma Gandhi eArchive and Reference Library website includes the quotation "You must be the change you wish to see in the world." Keyes indicates that "Gandhi's descendants say he made that observation in person."
7. Jeff Woods, "New Tasks for the New Congregation: Reflections on Congregational Studies," Resources for American Christianity, 2005, 1, www.resourcingchristianity.org.
8. Ibid., 5.
9. Ammerman, *Congregation and Community*.
10. Richard J. McCorry, *Dancing with Change: A Spiritual Response to Changes in the Church* (New York: iUniverse, 2004).
11. Ibid., 43.
12. Ibid., 53.

13. William Bridges, *Managing Transitions: Making the Most of Change* (Upper Saddle River, NJ: Addison Wesley, 1997).

14. Speed Leas, *Moving Your Church through Conflict* (Herndon, VA: Alban Institute, 1985).

15. An interest-based approach seeks to find win-win solutions that satisfy the underlying needs and interests of both parties, whereas a rights-based approach seeks to determine if a party's rights were violated and how that can be redressed. Either approach may be appropriate depending upon the nature of the conflict or complaint.

16. Parts of the discussion in this chapter regarding change and conflict were adapted from *The Little Book of Healthy Organization,* coauthored by David Brubaker and Ruth Zimmerman (Intercourse, PA: Good Books, 2009).

17. Adding a worship service, changing fellowship patterns, and initiating new community projects all correlated positively with growth in a linear regression model, but the correlations were not statistically significant.

Chapter 6
Where Do We Go from Here?

1. The ultimate fear of many local congregational leaders is that conflict will split the congregation. When a split, or schism, occurs a sizeable percentage of the congregation withdraws to form a new congregation or join other existing congregations. However, a true schism is a rarity at the local congregation level. Of the thirty congregations with which I have consulted since 1986, only three (10 percent) involved a genuine schism. This percentage is consistent with those reported by other congregational consultants with whom I have spoken.

2. The "200 barrier" is the best-known illustration of the hypothesis that congregations can get stuck within certain size categories. However, this hypothesis is now being questioned even in the popular literature, such as Kevin E. Martin's *The Myth of the 200 Barrier: How to Lead through Transitional Growth* (Nashville: Abingdon, 2005).

3. John Sutton and Mark Chaves, "Explaining Schism in American Protestant Denominations, 1890–1990," *Journal for the Scientific Study of Religion* 43, no. 2 (2004): 171–90.

4. John W. Meyer and Brian Rowan, "Institutionalized Organizations: Formal Structure as Myth and Ceremony," *The American Journal of Sociology* 83, no. 2 (Sept. 1977): 340–63.

5. Chaves, *Congregations in America*, 155.

6. This study did not establish whether the worship services were begun as a response to growth or out of a desire for growth. Though it seems reasonable to surmise that both mechanisms were at work within the sample, some respondents' comments indicated that a desire for growth was one motivator for adding a service.

7. Hipps, *Hidden Power of Electronic Culture.*

8. Whereas the lead pastor departed in only 25 percent of the "no conflict" cases, the lead pastor departed in 56 percent of the conflict cases. Thus conflict avoidance by leaders is understandable: conflict in the church makes it more than twice as likely the lead pastor will depart, according to this sample of congregations.

9. Schein, *Organizational Culture and Leadership*, 2.

10. Nancy Tatom Ammerman, Jackson W. Carroll, Carl S. Dudley, William McKinney, eds., *Studying Congregations: A New Handbook* (Nashville: Abingdon, 1998), 192.

11. Carl S. Dudley and Nancy T. Ammerman, *Congregations in Transition: A Guide for Analyzing, Assessing, and Adapting in Changing Communities* (San Francisco: Jossey-Bass, 2002), 10.
12. McCorry, *Dancing with Change.*
13. See David Brubaker, "Ordination and Conflict: A Comparative Case Study of Conflict over Ordination of Gays and Lesbians in 25 American Denominations" (master's thesis, University of Arizona, 2002).
14. An exception to this rule is when the presenting conflict has escalated to a high Level 4 or Level 5 on the Leas scale, in which case the first task of the intervener will be to deescalate the conflict to a level where genuine analysis can occur. Speed Leas discusses this in *Moving Your Church through Conflict.*
15. Most community- and court-based mediation programs in the United States document settlement rates of 70 to 80 percent for interpersonal mediation. By contrast, Speed Leas admits to a 53 percent success rate, albeit using four criteria that go beyond mere settlement.
16. The saying among congregational consultants that "the identified issue is never the real issue" indicates that many have learned from experience not to accept the parties' framing at face value.
17. Rendle, *Leading Change in the Congregation*, 3 (emphasis original).